EXPLORING JACKFRUIT FOR VALUE AND HEALTH BENEFITS

BY
ESTUTI CHANDRA

ABSTRACT

Jackfruit is the largest tree borne fruit having nutritional and health benefits. A study was conducted on value addition and therapeutic significance of jackfruit. A simple survey conducted in Sirsi district, Karnataka revealed that jackfruit was consumed daily from November to June. Further, three stages of jackfruit were researched. Highest moisture was found in ripe jackfruit (76.20%) whereas highest protein (4.36%) was present in mature jackfruit. The energy content (kcal) in the three stages were found to be 368, 374 and 357, mature having maximum and ripe having minimum. The calcium, iron, zinc and copper contents ranged from 36.75 to 55.30 mg/100g, 0.34 to 2.75 mg/100g, 0.09 to 2.44 and 0.20 to 2.00mg/100g respectively. The total starch, amylopectin and resistant starch contents were higher in mature jackfruits (40.50, 32.54 & 16.09%). Protein digestibility of mature jackfruit was (91%). Ripe jackfruit had significantly higher *IVSD* at 30 min (11.31%), 90 min (28.58%) and 120 min (40.51%). Inhibition of alpha glucosidase (95.60%) and alpha amylase (84.60%) was higher in immature stage. Lowest glycemic index was recorded in immature stage (47.66%) followed by mature (54.75%) and ripe (62.16%). Jackfruit flour was developed to formulate composite mix. Composite mix chapathi with jackfruit flour (30%) and wheat flour (70%) obtained highest scores for appearance (8.09), colour (8.50), flavour (8.77), taste (7.18), texture (7.14) and overall acceptability (8.50). The DPPH and phosphomolybdenum inhibition were significantly higher in composite mix (96.00% and 79.00%). The bacterial (2.72×10^2 and 2.67×10^2 CFU/g) and fungal (8.25×10^1 and 8.45×10^1 CFU/g) count increased up to 180th day of storage. *Escherichia* coli were not detected during storage. The glycemic index of composite mix was 40.82. Majority of diabetics (35.48%) liked the composite mix.

C O N T E N T S

CHAPTER -1

INTRODUCTION

Ancient Indians had a great sense of identity with flora and fauna, and were aware of the ecological balance found in nature. Valmiki's *Ramayana* is the most important source of botanical information. In Ramayana, Valmiki has accounted for both edible and non-edible types of vegetation like *bael* (Bengal quince), jackfruit, *can Dana* (Sandalwood tree), *nagakesara* (Cobras saffron, Ironwood tree), *sala* (Sal), *uddalaka* (Indian Cherry) and mangroves etc. in verse (5. 5.43, 38; 5.15.2, 3,115) (Amirthalingam, 2013).

The domesticated jackfruit tree, botanically known as *Artocarpus heterophyllus* Lam., is important in tropical and subtropical regions, particularly in South and Southeast Asia. The word *Artocarpus* is derived from two Greek words *artos* and *carpos* which mean bread and fruit while the word "jackfruit" finds its origin from the Portuguese term jaca, which in turn, is derived from the Malayalam word *chukka*. Jackfruit (*Artocarpus heterophyllus Lam.*) is the largest tree-borne fruit in the world, reaching up to 50 kg in weight and 60-90 cm in length. Recently, Sidhu, (2012) reported fruit weighing 81 kg from Panrutti, India. A fully grown tree produces around 700 fruits weighing 0.5 to 50 kg every year. Being a tropical fruit jackfruit is located in tropical, high rainfall, coastal and humid areas of the world. India is considered to be the native of jack fruit. It was cultivated in India 3000 to 6000 years ago and is found in almost all parts of the country except in desert areas. The fleshy carpel which is botanically the perianth is the edible portion.

Jackfruit is generally seed propagated and cross-pollinated, therefore much variation exists. Few commercial varieties have been selected for marketing purpose, but generally, two main types exist-soft flesh and crisp flesh. Jackfruit shows a considerable range of variation in morph agronomic.

A considerable variation between trees has been observed for traits such as growth habit, canopy structure, leaf size, fruit size, shape, colour, fruit bearing (age and seasonality) and maturity. Variation also exists in density, size and shape of spines on rind, fruit-bearing, sensory quality, flesh types, sweetness, flavour and taste (Azad, 2000).

An Indian variety bearing small fruits called Rudrakshi is found to have relatively smooth rind and inferior quality flesh. There is no well-defined variety in jackfruit and different types are known differently in different localities. Local selections have been named as Champa, Hazari (bearing more number of fruits in a tree) and Gulabi (rose-scented). Raw jackfruits have good demand in India as vegetable for culinary purpose, the emphasis is also given on fruit characters like the thickness of rind and softness of flesh at premature stage of fruit development. New selections, namely, NJT1, NJT2, NJT3 and NJT4 with large fruits and excellent pulp quality have been identified for table purpose, while types like NJC1, NJC2, NJC3, and NJC4 were found better for culinary purpose (Sidhu, 2012).

In South India (Kerala, Tamil Nadu, and Karnataka), different forms of jackfruit (Verica, Kosha, Navarikka) are available and the maximum diversity has been reported from Wynad Plateau of Western Ghats of Kerala.

In Uttar Pradesh, a large-fruited variety Kapa, locally known as Katha produces fruits as big as 40 kg in weight and the fruit is very sweet in taste on ripening. A small-fruited (2-8 kg) jackfruit variety known as Barka is used for pickle making and other culinary uses.

It is rightly called poor man's food in South-East Asia (Singh et al., 1963; Bose, 1985), as it constitutes the major portion of the diet of people as vegetable in unripe stage and as delicious nutritious fruit during the season. The jackfruit is a high yielding fruit crop which bears fruits all-round the year with peak production during the months of June and December. The main fruiting season is in summer, some fruit may ripen at other times, but usually not in winter and early spring.

Jackfruit has a green to yellow brown exterior rind that is composed of hexagonal, bluntly conical carpel apices that cover a thick, rubbery, and whitish to yellowish wall. It is a multiple aggregate fruit which is formed by the fusion of multiple flowers in an inflorescence. About 30 per cent of the fruit weight is occupied by the flesh. There are large number of bulbs inside the fruit, which have high nutritional value. The fruit is made up of three main portions. They are the fruit axis; the persistent perianth and the true fruit. Due to the presence of laticiferous cells that produce latex, which helps to hold the fruits together, the axis and the core of the fruit are inedible (Ranasinghe et. al. 2019).

All parts of jackfruit tree are equally important for human beings. Jack roots, spiny skin of fruit and bark of a tree are used in the textile industry for making dye; trunk and branches are used in the furniture industry. Leaves are used for fodder and are used in Konkan Indian kitchen as *idli* case. It is believed that *idli* cooked in jackfruit leaves gives immense flavor because of phytochemicals present in it. Jack fruit rind, pulp, and seeds are used for culinary purpose. Jackfruit is also used for further processing. For instance, jackfruit leather and jackfruit chips are being made commercially after hydration. The paste of jackfruit pulp is also manufactured into baby food, jam, jelly, candies, juice, marmalades, fruit-rolls, and ice cream. Advances in processing technologies have pushed towards more new products. Freeze-dried, vacuum-fried and cryogenic processing are new methods of preservation for modern jackfruit products.

Nutritionally jackfruit is a good source of vitamin C, fibre, carbohydrates, and antioxidants. It is also rich in vitamin B, potassium, calcium, iron and proteins. Affordable and readily available supplement to our staple food are its seeds which are rich in proteins and can be relished as a nutritious nut. The fruit is also the source of chemical "Jacalin" useful in preventing colon cancer, AIDS, *etc.* Unripe fruit could also help to control diabetes. Indeed, it has a higher hypoglycaemic effect than some antidiabetic drugs. So much so that diabetic patients who make use of the reasonably good quantity of unripe jackfruit can cut down their insulin intake by 50 per cent (Anon, 2020).

Phytochemical studies have shown that jackfruit contains useful compounds like prenylflavones, sterols, and flavonoids which may have been responsible for the various pharmacological properties. In Ayurveda, it is reported to possess antibacterial, anti-inflammatory, antidiabetic, antioxidant and immunomodulatory properties. It is an important source of bioactive compounds like isoartocarpin, cyloartocarpin, morin, dihydromorin, cynomacurin, artocarpin, oxydihydroartocarpesin,heterophylol, artocarpetin, norartocarpetin, betulinic acid, cycloartinone,artocarpesin and artocarpanone which are useful to treat wounds, fever, boils, skin diseases, diuretic, constipation, ophthalmic disorders, snakebite and convulsions etc. (Zheng 2009)

Jackfruit is harvested at different stages of maturity depending on its use and market demand. Jackfruit is such fruit which can be harvested at any stage after 15-20th day of anthesis. It is used as a vegetable, pickle, and in preparation of many Indian traditional cuisines like jack-*biryani*, shredded jack stuffed *parantha etc.* at very immature stage, where fruitlets (bulbs) or seeds are not yet fully developed. They are dark green with hard, stiff and closely spaced spines. The testa (exocarp) of the seeds is not yet formed; hence there is no need of removing the testa while preparing them for use as vegetables. The seeds at this stage are still very tender and tasty. In the second stage, fully developed fruitlets and seeds are used for making various preparations like curries. A dull, hollow sound observed when the fruit is tapped which is considered to be the most reliable indicator of maturity. Harvesting at this stage permits the fruit to be used for making chips, various curries, *papad, dosa idli* etc. In third stage ripe fruits are preferred, they can be also picked at the mature stage when they emit the jackfruit's characteristic aroma. This stage is used for many local food preparations like *holige, modak* etc.

Post-harvest processing of jackfruit is the tough task to perform. Fruit is cut into half and left for few minutes for latex to ooze out, vegetable oil smeared hands and knives are used to clean the latex and then manually bulbs are separated. This process is time and energy consuming. Recent research has evolved novel technologies to reduce human drudgery in post harvest processing of the fruit, like peeling of young jackfruit, cutting or separating bulbs. Currently, processed and packed young jackfruit and its bulbs can be found in stores as ready to cook or ready to eat product.

Jackfruit is also therapeutically rich fruit, as it is said that one cup of jackfruit will fulfill 11 per cent of daily requirement of fibre of human body.

Diabetes mellitus is a chronic metabolic disorder characterized by disturbances in carbohydrate, lipid and protein metabolism and if uncontrolled leads to complications like retinopathy, nephropathy, neuropathy and microangiopathy. Haematological coma and hepato-renal disturbances can occur because of currently available synthetic antidiabetic agents. Diabetes mellitus affects five per cent of the world population. An inherited or acquired deficiency of insulin secretion results in an increased blood glucose level, which in turn produces adverse effects on different body systems. It requires continuing patient self-management and medical care to prevent acute complications and reduce the risk of long-term complications.

Evidence suggests that inflammation is the underlying cause of the long term complications resulting from uncontrolled diabetes. A diet high in antioxidant rich foods can help to overcome inflammation in the body. Foods contain various proportions of well-known macronutrients and the micronutrients, vitamins, fiber, minerals, and electrolytes; as well as several hundred naturally occurring substances in plant foods called phytochemicals. India is a land of herbal products and plant-based vegetarian diets. Wider acceptance of the medicinal value of foods and their use will cut down the health care costs as well. It is need of the hour to pay attention to underutilized food to prevent diabetes and its complications.

It is evident that jackfruit is rich in many nutritional and health promoting components. However inadequate information is available on variation in biochemical constituents of dietary significance of fruit at different stage of maturity and to fulfil the expectations of diabetic sufferers, various research have been conducted on fruits and vegetables. Thus this "poor man's" fruit was taken for the present study and planned to evaluate the nutritional quality characteristics of jackfruit at different stage of maturity and to test the therapeutic benefits with following objectives.

1. To estimate the nutrient composition of jackfruit at different stages of maturity

2. To find out the antioxidant activity of jackfruit at various stages of maturity

3. To design and develop anti-diabetic composite mix

4. To characterize the developed product for Glycemic Index, nutritional, sensory, microbial and storage quality

5. To test the efficacy of developed product among diabetic population.

CHAPTER -2

REVIEW OF LITERATURE

A comprehensive review of literature is an essential part of any scientific investigation. The review of literature leads the researcher to conclude findings with source to past studies. A brief account of the research conducted on value addition and therapeutic significance of fruits with special source to jackfruit (*Artocarpus heterophyllus*) has been reviewed and presented under the following heads:

2.1 Physical parameters of jackfruit

2.2 Physico-chemical parameters and functional properties of jackfruit

2.3 Proximate composition and mineral content of jackfruit

2.4 Antioxidant activity, bioactive compounds and antimicrobial property of jackfruit

2.5 Antidiabetic effect and glycemic index of jackfruit and its parts

2.6 Effect of Processing on jackfruit and its parts

2.7 Value addition to jackfruit

2.8 Development of composite flour

2.9 Storage quality of composite flour

2.10 Glycemic effect of composite flour

2.1 Physical parameter of jackfruit

The Physical parameters including appearance, colour, weight, volume, circumference and others influence marketability and acceptance of the fruits by public.

Mitra and Mani (2000), Reddy *et al.* (2004), Jagadeesh *et al.* (2007), Prakash *et al.* (2009) and Mushumbusi (2015) studied physical properties of jackfruit. The length of fruits ranged from 22 to 90 cm and breadth from 13 to 50 cm. Individual fruits weighed between two to 20 kg, with highest weight recorded to be of about 50 kg. Jackfruits have green to yellow brown peel, which was composed of hexagonal, bluntly conical carpel apices. It was reported to be multiple aggregate fruit formed by the fusion of multiple flowers in an inflorescence. About 30 per cent of the fruit weight was occupied by the flesh.

Haq (2006) in his book mentioned, jackfruits were roundish, having width of 7.5-12.5 cm, thickly set with stiff conical spines, greenish yellow becoming dull orange on ripening. The stalks were 1-1.5 cm long, sunk in the fruit. The pulp was yellow and had a sweet, pleasant flavour.

Jagadeesh *et al.* (2010) conducted a survey of coastal zone of Karnataka and attempted to account for the natural variability present in physical parameters of bulbs of jackfruits. A significant variation in physical parameters of jackfruit bulbs was observed among the 30 jackfruit selections surveyed and studied. Mean values of bulb characters and bulb colour in dessert type jackfruit selections showed, fruit mass to be 3.52 kg per fruit, bulb mass 1.54 kg per fruit. Weight of single bulb was 21.19 g, length 5.03 cm, breadth 3.10 cm, flake mass 1.60 kg, flake thickness 0.350 cm, bulb colour was light yellow. Edible portion was 30.17 per cent, seed was 13.54 per cent, average number of seeds was 72.67 and seed mass was 0.477 kg per fruit.

Jonathan *et al.* (2013) stated that jackfruit is a multiple fruit composed of the coherence of multiple flowers. Fruit was moderately large to very large, weighing around 4.5-27.3 kg. A few cultivars were small fruited, weighing 1.4 to 4.5 kg. Fruit skin color was green when immature and green, greenish-yellow to brownish yellow when ripe. The inside of the fruit contained the edible, sweet, aromatic, crispy, soft or melting pulp that surrounded each seed. Between the seeds and edible pulp was the inedible "rag". Pulp color varied from amber to yellow, dark yellow, or orange. Seeds were long or oval in shape, the number per fruit varied from 30 to 500. The time from flowering to fruit maturity ranged from 150 to 180 days.

Ibrahim *et al.* (2013) studied the physical parameters of freshly harvested jackfruits of 10 cultivars (AH001 to AH010) procured from three gardens. The results showed that colours of bulbs were found to be light yellowish (AH002), yellowish (AH003) and orange (AH004). The maximum fruit weight recorded was 5.70 kg (AH003) which was followed by 3.80 kg (AH006). The rind percentage ranged from 15.67 to 22.73 per cent, the peel percentage varied from 14.86 to 23.68 per cent. Total wastage (rind, rags and seed coat) percentage varied from 38.33 to 46.04 per cent.

While studying the physical parameters of jackfruit, Wangchu *et al.* (2013) reported that length of fruit ranged from 19.00 to 58.50 cm, and diameter from 13.77 to 24.17 cm. Fruit weight ranged from 1.6 kg to 16.47 kg while the weight of fruit rind ranged from

736.67g to 5.4 kg. Number of bulbs per kg of fruit were 6 to 60.33 and weight of each bulb ranged from 254.67 to 610.00 g. Bulb length ranged from 3.60 to 8.30 cm. Flake width was 2.13 to 6.80 cm. Number of seeds/kg of fruit was found to be 27.42 to 60.00. Weight of 100 seeds ranged from 263.33 g to 1.13 kg.

Krishnan *et al.* (2015) conducted study on physico-chemical properties of various genotypes of jackfruit collections from Kerala. Individual fruit weight ranged from 1.69 to17.50 kg, bulb mass 0.80 - 10.25 kg/per fruit, flake mass 0.64 – 6.62 kg, single bulb weight 13.20 - 48.36 g and flake thickness 0.31 - 0.63 cm.

Rupnawar *et al.* (2016) mentioned that the average weight of unripe jackfruit weighed on an average 7-10 kg, the length and diameter were 40.4 cm and 32.35 cm respectively which were reduced by about 20 per cent on ripening. Bulb, seed and rind components of ripe fruit were 47, 10 and 53 per cent, respectively. The weight of unripe fruit bulb was 16.67 g and of ripe bulbs was 11.77 g. The volume of unripe bulb was 16.80 cm^3 and that of ripe bulb were 11.44 cm^3. The bulk density of the unripe fruit bulbs was 0.992g/cm^3 and ripe bulbs were 1.029 g/cm^3, each seed of jackfruit weighed 3.88 g, volume and bulk density were 3.51 cm^3 and 1.10 g/cm^3. Jackfruit was classified into three sizes based on length 28-34 cm as small, 35- 45 as medium and more than 45 cm in length as large size fruits.

Goswami and Chacrabati (2016) mentioned that jackfruit was oblong to cylindrical in shape and typically 30–40 cm in length, although it reaches 90 cm sometimes. Jackfruits may weigh 4.5 to 30 kg (commonly 9–18 kg), with a maximum reported weight of 50 kg. The exterior of the fruit is green, turning to yellow when ripe. The interior consists of large edible bulbs of yellow, banana-flavoured flesh that encloses a smooth, oval, light-brown seed. After 3–8 months of flowering, the fruits become matured. The seeds are recalcitrant. Usually a change of fruit color from light green to yellow indicates maturity. Furthermore, there is a dull, hollow sound when the fruit is tapped. Cold storage trials indicate that ripe fruits can be kept for 3-6 weeks at 11-13°C and relative humidity of 85-95 per cent.

The variability in physico-chemical characteristics of 13 fully mature and ripened jackfruit genotypes from Maharashtra was studied by Ningot *et al.* (2018). The average fruit weight ranged from 1.18 kg to 5.10 kg, total flake weight per fruit ranged from 0.11kg to 0.38 kg, number of bulbs per fruit ranged from 17 to 159.33, seed weight ranged from 0.3 g to

10.71 g and bulb weight from 2.33 g to 30.3 g. Colour of flakes were between pale yellow to orange yellow.

Rana *et al.* (2018) conducted research on two varieties of tender jackfruit (hard and soft variety). The tender jackfruit was divided into four stages. The various stages were decided on the basis of use of tender jackfruits for different products such as pickle, vegetables, chips and other value added products. In hard variety, there was a significant increment of 121.12, 46.09 and 75.93 per cent in the weight, length, and diameter, respectively, from stage one to four. Respective, increment of 60.80, 57.63 and 119.77 per cent was observed in the soft variety. For both the varieties the sphericity decreased with increase in stages (P\0.05). The fruit of hard variety of one and two stage possessed sphericity values of 0.91 and 0.89, respectively, which decreased to 0.83 at stage four. The sphericity values for soft variety in stage one and four were 0.78 and 0.89, respectively. Percentage of edible matter for both hard and soft variety were 63.41 and 66.45per cent at stage one, and it decreased to 12.36 and 21.17 per cent, respectively, at stage four.

Jackfruit is one of the largest fruits in the world, there are more than 40 cultivars available across the globe. The fruit were used in different levels of maturity, with maturity changes could be seen in shape, size, color, smell, texture, weight diameter and height.

2.2 Physico-chemical parameters and functional properties of jackfruit

Physico-chemical parameters like titrable acidity, pH, total soluble solids, total suspended solids etc. play an important role during preparation, processing and storage besides the sensory characteristics of food.

Reddy *et al.* (2004) worked on physico-chemical characteristics of jackfruit clones of south Karnataka. Different accessions were identified to study fruit characters. TSS recorded more variability in the clones identified and ranged from 24.8 - 40.5° brix, with highest value in ACC No 18. Lowest acidity (0.18%) was noticed in Acc.No.7 respectively. Reducing sugar was more in Acc.No.15 (8.62%).

Souza *et al.* (2009) reported that ripe jackfruit pulp contained high ash (3.71%), low pH (4.82), high soluble solids (23.00 Brix°) and titrable acidity (1.04%).

Jagadeesh *et al.* (2010) conducted a survey of coastal zone of Karnataka and accounted for variability in physico-chemical qualities of jackfruit bulbs. A significant variation in physio-chemical characters of jackfruit bulbs was observed among the 30 jackfruit selections surveyed in this zone. Results showed titratable acidity of 0.296 per cent, TSS of 24.14 °brix, TSS: acid ratio of 89:46, total sugars 20.98 per cent, reducing sugars 8.45 per cent, starch 2.23 per cent and carotenoids of 0.536 mg/100g on an average of 30 selections.

Goswami *et al.* (2011) determined the physico chemical composition of three types of jackfruits (*Khaja, Dorsaha and Ghila*) collected from two places Madhopur and Valuka. Results have shown that the higher pH in *Khaja, Dorsaha* and *Ghila* was 6.45, 5.82 and 5.61. Titrable acidity of *Ghila* and *Khaja* pulps was 0.91 per cent and 46 per cent respectively. *Khaja* and *Ghila* contained (13.80%) and (15.27 %) total sugar. Total soluble solid was 27.0 per cent in *Dorsaha* whereas in *Ghila* it was 19.3 per cent. Jackfruit pulps from Valuka *Khaja, Ghila* and *Dorasha*, Modhupur *Khaja* and *Ghila* had 7.37, 6.11, 7.07, 8.34 and 7.27 per cent starch.

Krishnan *et al.* (2015) conducted study on physico-chemical properties of jackfruit collections from Kerala. Fully mature fruits were collected and allowed to ripen at room temperature. The chemical parameters varied significantly among these selected genotypes. The TSS varied from 12.60 to 31.80 °Brix, ascorbic acid 1.50 to10.55 mg/100g, acidity 0.20 to1.02 per cent, total sugar 20.84 to 61.88 per cent and reducing sugar from 3.18 to9.39 per cent.

Borgis (2017) conducted study on physical properties of seed were recorded and processed employing: boiling, pressure cooking, pan roasting, microwave roasting and baking and found that each seed was 3.52 cm long, 1.77 cm wide and 1.27 cm thick, on an average weight of each seed was 5.47 g, volume 5.25 ml and bulk density 1.06 g/ml. Boiled seeds were highly acceptable with acceptability index of 83.15. Flour yield was significantly higher in unprocessed seeds (42.17 ± 0.06%) followed by dry processing. Processing significantly increased bulk density of flour. Water absorption capacity (282.71 and 260.30%), swelling capacity (6.46 and 6.24%) and solubility (21.07 and 20.51%) were significantly higher in wet processed flour whereas oil absorption capacity was significantly higher in dry processing (115.80 - 164.76%).

The variability in physico-chemical characteristics of 13 jackfruit genotypes was studied by Ningot *et al.* (2018) from Maharashtra. They collected fully mature and ripened fruits of jackfruit. Physiochemical parameters, like TSS ranged from 14.07 to 27.53 °Brix, titrable acidity from 0.09 to 1.05 per cent, total sugar from18.95 to 32.53 per cent, and reducing sugars from 14.44 to 24.98 per cent.

Rana *et al.* (2018) conducted research on two varieties of tender jackfruit (hard and soft variety). The tender jackfruit were divided into four stages. In soft variety total solids content was 0.18, 0.20, 0.22 and 0.22 per cent at first, second, third and fourth stage. pH was respectively 6.78, 6.06, 6.44, and 6.56, TSS was 2.70, 4.90, 6.30, 7.10 °B and TDS 1.03, 1.11, 2.66 and 2.53 ppm. In Hard variety pH was 6.08, 6.21, 6.13 and 6.11in all four stages. TSS was 1.50, 2.40, 2.80 and 5.10. °B and TDS was 1.22, 1.73, 1.96 and 2.33 ppm respectively.

Ranasinghe and Marapana (2019) worked on effect of maturity stage on physico-chemical properties of jackfruit (*Artocarpus heterophyllus* Lam.) flesh. Jackfruits of four maturity stages including immature stage (67 weeks), immature stage (8-10 weeks), mature stage (12-14 weeks) and fully ripen stage (14-16 weeks). Results indicated that the total soluble solids increased with maturity from 3.4 to 19.6 per cent, corresponding to the increase of total sugar content. pH increased from the immature stage (5.27) to the mature stage (6.25), then decreased to 5.76 during ripening, while the titratable acidity decreased from 0.17 - 0.29 per cent.

Ibrahim *et al.* (2013) conducted experiment using freshly harvested jackfruits of ten cultivars AH001 to AH010. Maximum moisture content (76.62%) was found in cultivar AH006 with minimum dry matter (23.38%). The total soluble solids and pH ranged from 18.80 to 27.30 per cent and 4.53 to 4.75 respectively. Total sugar content was found to be highest (17.01%) in AH001 and lowest (11.84%) in AH003. Maximum reducing and non-reducing sugar contents (4.59 and 12.42%) were found in AH001. The highest vitamin C content (31.55 mg/100g) was found in cultivar AH010 and minimum (17.82 mg/100g) in AH008. Highest acidity (0.075% as citric acid) was observed in AH009 followed by AH008 (0.068% as citric acid), whereas AH005 had the lowest acidity (0.037% as citric acid). Ash content of different jackfruit cultivars ranged from 0.403 to 1.276 per cent.

The chemical component of jackfruit *viz.*, pH, total soluble solids, total dissolved solids, total sugars, reducing sugar, starch etc. changes with maturity.

2.3 Proximate composition and mineral content of jackfruit

Carbohydrate, protein, fat, ash, fibre (crude and dietary) etc. are basic components of any food after water. They help in growth and maturity of food and differ at many stages of cultivation. These components help in the development of many other beneficial phytochemicals, enzymes and antioxidants within the food. Jackfruit also contains good amount of these nutrients which makes it a miraculous fruit.

Young jackfruit contained 76.2-85.2 g moisture, 2.0-2.6 g protein, 0.1-0.6 g fat, 9.4-11.5 g carbohydrate, 2.6-3.6 g fibre, 0.9 g total minerals and 50-210 kJ of energy. Calcium 30.0-73.2 mg, magnesium 27 mg, phosphorus 20.0-57.2 mg, potassium 287-323 mg, sodium 3.0-35.0 mg and iron 0.4-1.9 mg were the minerals present in jackfruit. The fruit contained considerable amount of vitamin A - 30 IU, thiamine- 0.05-0.15 mg, riboflavin- 0.05–0.2 mg and vitamin C- 12.0-14.0 mg. Nutrients in ripe jackfruit ranged from 72.0-94.0 g moisture, 1.21.9 6 g protein, 0.1-0.4 g fat, 16.0-25.4 g carbohydrate, 1.0-1.5 g fibre, 20.6 g total sugars, 0.87-0.9 g total minerals, 88-410 kJ energy, 20.0-37.0 mg calcium, 54 mg magnesium, 38.0-41.0 mg phosphorus, 191- 407 mg potassium, 2.0- 41.0 mg sodium and 0.5-1.1 mg iron per 100 g. vitamin A 175-540 IU, thiamine 0.03-0.09 mg, riboflavin 0.050.4 mg and vitamin C 7.0-10.0 mg were the vitamins present in ripe jackfruit. (Narasimham, 1990; Soepadmo, 1992, Gunasena *et al.*, 1996; Azad, 2000; Haq, 2006).

Jagtap *et al.* (2010) analysed chemical composition of young and ripe jackfruit. Result showed that every 100g of young and ripe jackfruit contained, moisture (76.2-85 and 72.0-94.0 g), protein (2.0-2.6 and 1.2-1.9 g), fat (0.1-0.6 and 01-04 g) carbohydrate (9.4-11.5 and 16.0-25.4 g), fibre (2.6-3.6 and 1.0-1.5 g), total sugars (20.6), total minerals (0.9 and 0.87-0.9 g), energy (50-210 and 88-410 kj) respectively. Calcium was 30.0-73.2 and 20.0-37.0 mg/100g, magnesium was not found in young fruit but ripe fruit contained 27 mg/100g, phosphorous was 20.0-57.2 and 38.0-41.0 mg /100g, potassium was 287-323 and 191-407 mg/100g, sodium was 3.0-35.0 and 2.0-41.0 mg/100g, iron 0.4-1.9 and 0.5-1.1 mg/100g. Vitamin A (30 and 175-540 IU/100 g), thiamine (0.05-0.15 and 0.03-0.09 mg/100g), riboflavin (0.05-0.2 and 0.05-0.4 mg/100g)and vitamin C (12.0-14.0 and 7.0-10.0 mg/100g) were the vitamins found in young and ripe jackfruit respectively.

Goswami *et al.* (2011) undertook a study to determine chemical composition of three types of jackfruits (*Khaja, Dorsaha and Ghila*) collected from two different places (Vakula and

Modhupur). Every 100 g of Valuka Khaja contained 82.88 per cent moisture, 0.98 per cent ash, and 0.57 per cent protein, and 0.55 percent fibre, 5.20 mg per cent vitamin C, 334.06 μg/100 g carotene. Vakula *Ghila* had 84.44 per cent moisture, 1.04 per cent ash, 0.67 per cent protein, 0.60 per cent fibre, 7.26 per cent vitamin C and 470.91μg/100g of carotene. Valuka *Dorosha* contained 80.04 per cent moisture, 1.11 per cent ash, 0.91 per cent protein, 0.61 per cent fibre, 8.18 mg per cent vitamin C and 380.45 μg/100g carotene. Modhupur *Khaja* had 80.95 per cent moisture, 0.88 per cent ash, 0.83 per cent protein, 0.90 per cent fibre, 4.57 mg per cent Vitamin C, 346.03 μg/100g carotene. Modhupur *Ghila* showed 79.62 per cent moisture, 0.70 per cent ash, 0.97 percent protein, 0.51 per cent fibre, 7.13 mg per cent vitamin C and 520.46 μg/100g carotene.

Every 100g of edible part of ripe fruit contained 72–77.2 per cent moisture, 98 kcal energy, 1.3-1.9 g protein, 0.2 g fat, 15.1-25.4 g carbohydrate, 1-5 g fibre, 0.8-2.2 g ash (Love and Paul, 2011). Calcium (22-37 mg), iron (0.5–1.7 mg), phosphorus (38.0 mg), potassium (292-407 mg), sodium (2-48 mg) were the minerals found in ripe jackfruit. Vitamins presents in ripe fruit were vitamin C (8-10 mg), thiamine (0.03 mg), riboflavin (0.06 mg), niacin (0.4-4 mg), and vitamin A (540 IU) per 100 g.

USDA National Nutrient Database, (Anon 2010, 2011) states that ripe jackfruit contained good amount of macronutrients, (73.23 per cent moisture, 1.74g protein, 94 kcal energy, 0.3g fat and 2.6g fibre per 100 g) and micronutrients (303.00 mg potassium, 34.00 mg phosphorous, 36.00 mg calcium, 0.6mg iron per 100 g).

Moisture (84.0 and 77.2%), carbohydrate (9.4 and 18.9g), protein (2.6 and 1.9g), fat (0.3 and 0.1g), fibre (4.4 and 1.1g), total mineral matter (0.9 and 0.8g), calcium (50.1 and 20.0 mg), phosphorus (97.0 and 30.0 mg), iron (1.5 and 500.1mg), potassium (206.0 and 350.0mg), vitamin A (0.0 and 540.0 IU), thiamine (0.2 and 30.0 mg), riboflavin (0.1 and 0.1 mg), nicotinic acid (0.2 and 0.4 mg), vitamin C (11.0 and 7.0 mg), calorific value 50.0 and 84.0 kcal, were reported in tender and ripe jackfruit respectively. (Anon, 2012).

While analysing the chemical composition of jackfruit Pirasath *et al.* (2012) reported moisture content of 78.40 per cent, fat of 0.2 per cent, soluble protein of 0.03 per cent, total protein of 1.49 per cent and total dietary fiber of 4.81 per cent.

It is reported in the technical bulletin no.41 (jackfruit) of ICAR (Devi *et al.* 2014) that every 100g of ripe jackfruit contained 76.20 per cent moisture, 1.90 protein, 88 kcal energy,

0.10 g fat, 1.1g fibre, 19.80 g carbohydrates, 107.00 mg potassium, 20.00 mg calcium , 41.00 mg phosphorous, 0.56 mg iron and 175.00 β carotene.

Study conducted by Madalageri (2015) on various fruits including jackfruit showed that jack contains good amount of micro and macro nutrients (64.00 per cent moisture, 1.40 g protein, 92 Kcal energy, 1.62g fat, 18.05g carbohydrate, 0.36 mg zinc, 17.46 mg calcium, 36.53 mg phosphorous, and 0.29 mg iron per 100 g).

Proximate composition and mineral contents of unripe mature jackfruit flesh was evaluated by Begum (2018). Jackfruits were collected from different areas of Chattogram district of Chhattisgarh and named as JF_A to JF_J. Jackfruit flesh of JF_A had the highest moisture content (84.68± 0.01%) whereas jackfruit of JF_B had the lowest value (70.36±0.02 %). The highest value of ash (1.22±0.02 %) was found in JF_C and the lowest value (0.79±0.01 %) was in JF_D. Protein was higher (2.766 ±0.001%) in JF_C whereas lower value (0.795±0.02 %) was found in JF_E. In case of crude fiber, JF_A contained highest value (2.69±0.05%) and JF_E had lowest value (0.78±0.01%). Carbohydrate content (25.92±0.2 %) was higher in the JF_B. Among all jackfruits, sodium ranged from 32.67 mg/dl in JF_E to 22.88 mg/dl in JF_F, potassium ranged from 105.3 mg/dl in JF_J to 50.76 mg/dl JF_C, calcium (mg/dl) ranged from 20.14 in JF_D to 14.68 in JF_I, magnesium (mg/dl) ranged from 35.75 in JF_G and 31.14 in JG_D, chloride (mg/dl) ranged from 0.568 in JF_J to 0.324 in JF_C. Zinc (mg/dl) ranged from 0.568 in JF_H to 0. 224 in JF_B.

Rana *et al.* (2018) evaluated two varieties of tender jackfruit (hard and soft variety) at four stages. As the fruit maturity increased from stage 1 to 4, there was a significant decrease in vitamin A and C from 39.4 ± 3.6 to 27.0 ± 3.1 IU and 18.65 ± 0.24 to 12.06 ± 0.68 mg, respectively in hard variety. Whereas carbohydrates, calcium, sodium, phosphorus, potassium, energy values showed a significant increase from 54.6 to 57.5 g, 1.46 to 43.6 mg, 26.1 to 22.8 mg, 254.4 to 412.6 mg and 159.1 to 444.8 kJ respectively. The other components like fat (0.14 to 0.61± 0.12g), fibre (4.4 ± 0.1g), protein (2.1 to 2.6± 0.78g) and mineral (0.80 to 0.90mg) content did not show any significant change with various stages of the jackfruit. Similarly in soft variety with increase in maturity from stage 1 to 4 there was a significant decrease in vitamin A and C from 44.4 to 22.5 IU and 12.12 to 7.04 mg, respectively. Whereas carbohydrates, calcium, sodium, phosphorus, potassium, energy values shown a significant (P\0.05) increase from 19.6 ± 0.5 to 25.8 ± 0.3 g, 43.8 ± 1.8 to 57.5 ± 1.6, 12.1 ±

0.38 to 43.6 ± 0.93, 2.3 ± 0.6 to 22.8 ± 1.6, 190.6 ± 4.5 to 412.6 ± 4.9 mg, and 312.8 ± 22.4 to 444.8 ± 39.6 kJ, respectively. The other components like fat (0.922 to 0.44 ± 0.11g), fibre (2.1 to 2.3 ± 0.1g), protein (1.1 to 1.9g) and mineral (0.70 mg) content did not show any significant change with maturity of jackfruit.

2.4 Antioxidant activity, bioactive compounds and antimicrobial property of jackfruit

The substances that prevent or retard oxidation of biomolecules like proteins, lipids and DNA are called 'antioxidants'. Phenolic compounds constitute the most abundant class of antioxidants with an estimated total dietary intake as high as 1 g/day, which is 10 times higher than the intake of vitamin C and 100 times that of vitamin E.

The bioactive compounds - ascorbic acid, total phenolic, flavonoids and carotenoids were determined in ripe jackfruit pulp obtained from Brazil, (Barreto et al., 2009). The free radical scavenger activity was evaluated by the ABTS assay. Results showed that jackfruit contained 1.0 ± 0.0 mg /100g ascorbic acid, 34.1 ± 1.0 mg GAE/100 g of total phenols, 18.3 ± 2.9 mg CE/100 g of total flavonoids, 0.3 ± 0.0 mg/100 g total carotenoids. The free radical scavenger activity was 50 ± 3 mmol L^{-1} /100 g TEACb.

The antioxidant capacity of jackfruit (*Artocarpus heterophyllus*Lam. Fam. Moracae) pulp (JFP) obtained from Western Ghats India was determined by evaluating the scavenging activity using 1,1-diphenyl2- picrylhydrazyl (DPPH), ferric reducing power assays (FRAP) and N, N-dimethyl-p-phenylendiamine (DMPD) radical cation decolorization assay (Jagtap *et al.*, 2010). JFP was analyzed for total phenolic content (TPC) and total flavonoids content (TFC). Further the solvents were evaluated for extraction. Results revealed that ethanol (0.46±0.014 mg/GAE/G) was the best solvent for extracting total phenolic compounds, followed by water (0.25±0.017mg/GAE/G), methanol (0.21±0.012 mg/GAE/G) and acetone (0.18±0.012 mg/GAE/G). Acetone (60.19±0.02 mg RE/g) was best solvent for extraction of total flavonoids followed by water (1.20±0.020 mg RE/g), ethanol (20.23±0.0 mg RE/g) and methanol (0.24±0.01 mg RE/g). The DPPH radical scavenging effects of all extracts of JFP showed 50 per cent reduction of free radicals. The minimum and maximum IC50 values were 0.4 mg/ml and 0.7 mg/ml for methanolic extract. The ferric reducing power of JFP extracts increased with increase in concentration (1–5 mg/ml). The ferric reducing power of JFP extract (5 mg/ml) showed higher ability to reduce Fe^{3+} to Fe^{2+} ,1.7 mM TEAC g–1 for methanolic and 1.4 mM TEAC g–1 for water extract. The DMPD assay of JFP extracts which cause 50% inhibition (IC50) were as follows: 3.43 mg/ml of methanolic extract, 3.6 mg/ml of ethanolic extract and 3.9 mg/ml of water extract. It was observed that all JFP extracts exhibited lower free radical scavenging activity than the standard ascorbic acid.

Almeida *et al.* (2011) analysed for phenolics, vitamin C, anthocyanin contents and antioxidant activity of jackfruit. Fruits were collected from natural habitats, in the city of Fortaleza, Brazil. At least 10 fruits were combined for each of the three replicated samples. Antioxidant activity was evaluated from the extracts while fresh fruit pulps were used for analysis of total anthocyanin, total phenol, antioxidant activity and ascorbic acid. Results showed that, jackfruit contained 1.2±0.0 mg /100 g of ascorbic acid, 0.46±0.00 mg TA/100 g of total anthocyanin and 29.0±6.3mg GAE/100 g of total phenol. Antioxidant activity from ABTS and DPPH assay, against Trolox equivalent (μM of Trolox equivalents/g fresh mass) was 0.63±0.01 TEAC (μM/g), and 0.16±0.03 TEAC (μM/g) and from vitamin C equivalent was 9.39±0.18 VCEAC (mg/100 g) and 2.25±0.42 VCEAC (mg/100 g) respectively.

Biworo *et al.* (2015) observed antioxidant activity of aqueous extract of jackfruit. Fruits of were collected from Indonesia and seeds were separated. Fruits were washed with distilled water, cut into small pieces and blended. Ascorbic acid, beta-carotene and lycopene were determined. Hydroxyl radical and hydrogen peroxide scavenging activity and chelating effect of ferrous iron was measured to assess antioxidant activity. The highest phytochemical constituent in jackfruit extracts was ascorbic acid (0.44 mg/100ml) followed by beta-carotene (0.192 mg/100ml) and lycopene (0.072 mg/100ml). The highest antioxidant activity was scavenging hydroxyl radical activity (36.62%) followed by scavenging hydrogen peroxide (12.44%) and chelating of ferrous iron (7.98%).

Mature, senescent leaves, bulbs and seeds of *Artocarpus Heterophyllus* Lam. were collected from Achara village, Maharashtra to estimate polyphenols, flavonoids, DPPH action and reducing power (Gokhale *et al.*, 2015). Dried and powdered sample (1 g each) was mixed with 100 ml methanol to prepare extract. This methanolic extract was used for estimating antioxidant potential. Polyphenol contents were highest in senescent leaves (45 mg/g dwb) while flavonoids were highest in mature leaves (30 mg/g dwb). Polyphenol contents were found to be 10 mg/g dwb in bulb powder and flavonoids were 17 mg/g dwb. Among the bulb and seed flour, seed flour (60% inhibition) had higher antioxidant potential than bulb flour (50% inhibition).

Antioxidant activity (AA) of jackfruit extracts was evaluated by Pavan *et al.* (2014) using Trolox Equivalent Antioxidant Capacity (TEAC) and Oxygen Radical Absorbance Capacity (ORAC) method. Total phenol content (TPC) and flavonoid content (FC) were also assessed. TPC exhibited a significant increase in digested extract (33.9 ± 0.002 mg GAE/100 g) compared to undigested extracts (23.3 ± 0.004). Analysis by the TEAC method indicated that the antioxidant activity significantly increased from 56±0.005 to 318.4±0.014 mmol TE/100 g when digested. Similary, the ORAC values also increased significantly from 2115.95 ± 1.7 to 3560 ± 1.5 mmol TE/100 g with digestion of extracts.

Singh *et al.* (2015) conducted research to assess the phenolic acid content of skin, pulp and seed of raw and ripe jackfruit (*Artocarpus heterophyllus*). Results showed that raw fruit skin was rich in gallic acid (22.73 µg/g) followed by tannic and ferulic acids. In ripe fruit, the skin had high amount of ferulic (13.41 µg/g) and reduced amount of gallic acid (12.08 µg/g). The level of tannic acid (5.73 µg/g) was the same as that in raw fruit peel, whereas tannic acid was slightly high in ripe fruit peel. Flesh of raw fruit had all three phenolic acids where gallic acid (9.70±0.09 µg/g) was maximum followed by ferulic (8.04±0.07 µg/g) and tannic acids (4.78±0.05 µg/g). However, flesh of ripe fruit had high amount of gallic (19.31 µg/g) and low amount of ferulic (2.66 µg/g) acids. The raw pulp showed more phenolic acids than ripe fruit pulp. Four phenolic acids (gallic, tannic, caffeic and ferulic acids) were detected in raw fruit seeds where gallic acid (11.3 µg/g) was maximum followed by tannic (6.59 µg/g), caffeic (2.84 µg/g) and ferulic (2.38 µg/g) acids. There were only three phenolic acids in ripe jackfruit seed (gallilc, ferulic and tannic acids) in which gallic acid (11.3 µg/g) was maximum followed by ferulic (2.71 µg/g) and tannic acid (2.1 µg/g).

Studies have shown that jackfruit contained useful compounds like the flavonoids, sterols, phenols, tannins etc. which may have been responsible for the various pharmacological properties. The raw and ripe edible parts of jackfruits contain good amount of phenolic acids and thereby it signifies the importance in therapeutic activity for human health.

2.5 Antidiabetic effect and glycemic index of jackfruit

Glycemic index (GI) is the measure of immediate effect on blood glucose level after food consumption. Foods are classified into three categories based on glycemic index: low GI; ≤ 55, medium GI = 55-69, and high GI; ≥ 70. The low glycemic index foods are beneficial in management of disease conditions such as diabetes mellitus, obesity and cardiovascular disease etc. The glycemic index of fruit varies depending on the stage of harvest and their composition.

To determine the blood glucose response of jackfruit, a total of 38 healthy subjects randomly divided into groups of 12 to 20 subjects (mean age: 21.5+0.6 years, mean BMI: 21.13+1.49 kg/m^{-2}) were requested to consume test fruits or source food (glucose) after an overnight fasting on separate occasions (Yusof *et al.*, 2005). Test fruit and glucose contained 50g of carbohydrates. Finger-prick blood samples were obtained at 0 (fasting), 15, 30, 60, 90 and 120 min after consuming each fruit or glucose. The blood glucose response was obtained by calculating area under the curve (AUC). Jackfruit showed mean blood glucose 3.6+0.1mmol.min/L at 0 min, 4.6+0.2 mmol.min/L at 15 min, 5.7+0.1mmol.min/L at 30 min, 5.3+0.3 mmol.min/L at 60min, 3.8+0.2 mmol.min/L at 90 min, 3.7+0.2 mmol.min/L at 120 min. Area Under Curve for jackfruit was 127.94+15 mmol.min/L and for glucose was 313.27+10. Glycemic index of jackfruit was 41.

Jain *et al.* (2010) conducted the research to know the antidiabetic activity of aqueous extract of fruits of *Artocarpus heterophyllus*(AH) in alloxan induced type- II diabetes rats (n=6). Aqueous fruit extract (250 and 500 mg/kg or vehicle (gum acacia solution) or standard drug glibenclamide (0.25 mg/kg) were administered to the diabetic rats for 15 days. By retro-orbital puncture blood samples were collected and were analysed for serum glucose on 0, 5, 10 and 15th day using glucose oxidase-peroxidase reactive strips and a glucometer. In oral glucose tolerance test, glucose (2g/kg) was administered to non-diabetic control, glibenclamide (10 mg/kg) and extract treated rats. After glucose administration 0, 30, 60 and 120 min of the serum glucose levels were recorded. At 60th min rates on 500mg/kg of AH extract showed 93.50 mg/dl blood plasma level and those on glibenclamide drug induced showed that 91.50 mg/dl blood plasma level. The AH extract induced rats recorded 200.43 and 206.35 (mg/dl) of fasting blood glucose level in alloxan induced type- II diabetic rats on 10th and 15th days. Serum insulin levels also increased from 4.35 to 10.6 µU/ml in the treated group as compared to the control value. The treated groups showed a decrease in total cholesterol (125.33 to 94.00 mg/dl) and LDL cholesterol (149. 67 to 110. 67 mg/dl) and an increase in HDL cholesterol (17.23 to 41.33 mg/dl).

Anti-oxidative, hypolipidemic and hypoglycemic activities of jack fruit leaf extracts was estimated by Omar *et al.* (2011). The 70 per cent ethanol (JFEE), n-butanol (JFBE), water (JFWE), chloroform (JFCE), and ethyl acetate (JFEAE) extracts were obtained. The administration of JFEE or JFBE to streptozotocin induced diabetic rats significantly reduced fasting blood glucose from 200 to 56 and 79 mg/dl, respectively; elevated insulin from 10.8 to 19.5 and 15.1 µU/ml, respectively; decreased per cent glycosylated haemoglobin from 6.8 to 4.5 and 5.0.

Hettiaratchi *et al.* (2011) carried out a nutritional assessment of a composite jackfruit breakfast meal comprising of seeds (20%) and flesh (80%) employing healthy individuals (n=10, age: 20-30 years). The moisture content of the boiled jackfruit flesh was high (82% FW). Jack seeds contained 4.7 per cent protein (FW), 11.1per cent total dietary fibre and 8 per cent resistant starch on fresh weight basis. Jackfruit meal elicited a GI of 75(±11). The Glycemic Load of the normal serving size of the meal was medium. The slowly available glucose of jackfruit meal (30%) was twice that of the standard. The boiled jackfruit flesh contained disintegrated starch granules while seeds contained both intact swollen and disintegrated granules.

Premanath *et al.* (2011) determined the glycemic index of ripe jackfruit fifty gram of glucose and 50 g of available carbohydrate in the fruit was tested and the rate of rise of blood glucose levels at various intervals was recorded. The Glycemic Index of jackfruit was 63.

Pirasath *et al.* (2012) aimed to evaluate the glycemic index (GI) of ripe jackfruit. Healthy volunteers (20 nos.) of 21.05(±0.92) years, 53.90 (±9.36) kg body weights, 153.92 (±9.15) cm heights, and 20.55 (±2.22) BMI were fed with their written consent. Ripe jackfruit bulb (578.70 g) was fed to the volunteers which contained 75 g of carbohydrate. Glycemic response of jackfruit at 30 min was 39.50 (±8.02) and 60 min was 27.66 (±7.51). Glycemic index was 65.36.

The antidiabetic potential of jackfruit rags in high fat diet fed-low dose STZ induced type 2 diabetes rats was evaluated by Suchithra and Subramanian (2014). Phytochemical screening of the rag extract was performed. Diabetic rats were treated with jackfruit rag extract at a dosage of 300 mg/kg body weight daily for 30 days. Metformin (200 mg/kg. b.w) was used as a source drug. The levels of fasting blood glucose, plasma insulin and HbA1c were estimated. Intraperitoneal insulin tolerance test was performed. Rag extracts fed rats showed 134.93 mg/dl blood glucose level, 7.30 HBA1c, 12.34 µU/ml insulin and no sugar was found in urine. Those fed with metformin showed 119.70 mg/dl blood glucose level, 7.00 HBA1c, 14.50µU/ml insulin and no sugar in urine.

Biworo *et al.* (2015) observed anti-diabetic activity of aqueous extract of jackfruit. Fruits, were collected from Indonesia. Fruits without seeds were washed with distilled water, cut into small pieces and blended. Antidiabetic activity was determined by inhibition of haemoglobin glycation. From the result of study it was observed that increase of haemoglobin glycation concentration was followed by the increase of jackfruit extracts concentration. From this study it was also observed that the IC 50 of jackfruit extracts was 56.43 per cent.

The above studies indicate the anti-diabetic potential of jackfruit. Young jackfruit was having lower glycemic index compared to ripe jackfruit.

2.6 Effect of Processing on jackfruit

Okiliya *et al.* (2010) tested the applicability of solar drying, a popular method in the tropics, for processing of jackfruit leather. The effect of solar drying on the quality and consumer acceptability of jackfruit leather was compared to cabinet and convection oven drying methods. Solar drying was carried out in a greenhouse solar dryer for three days (average temperature of 36.7°C). Convection oven drying was carried out at 50°C for 18 hours. Results showed that the moisture content of solar dried leather (18.50 %) was not significantly different from that of cabinet dried leather (18.85 %). However, the moisture content of the leather dried using these methods was significantly higher than the oven dried leather (14.79 %). Solar dried leather had significantly lower color readings compared to cabinet dried leather but was not significantly different from oven dried leather. Instrumental results of texture showed that all the drying methods produced leathers with similar texture. Overall acceptability of the leathers was highest and were not significantly different for both cabinet (6.67) and oven (6.20) drying but lowest acceptability was received by solar dried leathers (4.47).

The effect of hot air oven and freeze drying on the jack fruit powder was investigated by Kumar *et al.,* (2012). Cleaned jackfruit bulbs (1kg) were dried in hot air oven at 60 °C for 30 hrs and yield obtained was 178 g/kg. For freeze drying the temperature was maintained at -40°C and vacuum was maintained at 86 m and dried for 40 hrs and the yield obtained was 160g/kg powder. Powders were stored in polyethylene bags and used for further analysis.

Results of the study showed that the Vitamin 'A' and 'C' contents in oven dried powder were 150.45 IU and 2.15 mg/100g and in freeze dried powder was 250.68 IU and 5.92 mg/100g. Juice was prepared using the powders and compared with fresh juice (Control). The sensory scores for color, taste, flavour of freeze dried jack fruit powder was on par with the fresh juice.

Rahman *et al.* (2012) standardized osmotic dehydration of jackfruit (*Artocarpus heterophyllus*) with varying sugar concentrations (35° 40° 45° 50°Brix). After osmosis the jackfruit pieces were spread over the trays and dried in cabinet drier and packed in high density polyethylene bags and stored at ambient temperature for a period of eight months. Minimum microbial count was observed when osmosed for osmosis in 50° Brix solution followed by 45° sugar solution. The retention of vitamin C, vitamin A (ß- carotene), total acid and total sugar was better for osmosis in 45° Brix solution followed by 50° Brix solution. The product of 45° Brix solution when stored for eight months at room temperature secured highest score for organoleptic evaluation and was ranked "like moderately" followed by the product of 50° Brix solution.

Saxsena *et al.* (2012) processed jackfruit (*Artocarpus heterophyllus L.*) bulbs minimally using variables such as $CaCl_2$ concentration (0.13–1.47%), ascorbic acid (AA) concentration (0.005–0.03%), and treatment time (8–43 min). Second-order polynomial model was proposed to use with regard to effect of independent variables on responses such as juice leakage, firmness, browning index, L value, and overall acceptability by response surface methodology (RSM) using a central-composite experimental design. The established models for responses showed a good fit with the experimental data (R2 > 0.896), describing the effect of independent variables on the quality parameters of minimally processed bulbs of jackfruit. The recommended processing conditions for maximizing firmness, L value and overall acceptability and minimizing juice leakage, and browning index in the samples at the end of 20 days of low temperature storage were found to be 0.02 per cent AA, one per cent $CaCl_2$ and 30 min of treatment time. The RSM was found to be an effective tool to model the effect of minimal processing treatments on the quality of jackfruit bulbs.

The effects of microwave vacuum and convective hot air dehydration of jackfruit (*Artocarpus heterophyllus*) bulbs on drying characteristics, rehydration ability and quality attributes was studied by Taiba *et al.* (2012). Jackfruit bulbs were dehydrated by microwave power output of 58, 140, 220, and 321W combined with vacuum level of -65 cmHg during microwave vacuum dehydration. Convective hot air dehydration was conducted with the hot air temperature of 60, 70, and 80°C. Microwave vacuum dehydration with power output of 321 W resulted in 133 times faster drying compared to convective hot air dehydration temperature of 60°C. Furthermore, microwave vacuum dehydration produced better quality dehydrated bulbs with higher rehydration ability and sensory attributes.

Ramli and Ahmed (2013) studied the effect of different calcium infusion methods on the texture and consumer acceptance of ripe jackfruit (*Artocarpus heterophyllus*) pulps. Calcium infusions were blanching, immersion and vacuum-assisted infusion at two levels of calcium concentration, (0.5% and 1.0% (w/v)). The blanched ripe pulps lost their texture after 3 days and exhibited "cooked" characteristic. The calcium-treated ripe pulps lost their texture slower than untreated pulps. The colour index indicated a darkening in all samples regardless of treatment. The ascorbic acid content of all the samples reduced during the 14 days of storage. Immersed ripe jackfruit pulps resulted in higher sinersis, followed by vacuum-assisted jackfruit pulps (ripe) and control. The cell walls and middle lamella of vacuum infused pulps were intact, while other samples showed sign of middle lamella dissolution. Based on textural characteristics and sensory evaluation, the ripe jackfruit pulps vacuum-infused with calcium at 1.0 per cent had better shelf life and there was significant increase in ascorbic acid (2.6mg/100g) compared to other treatments (1.8mg/100g).

Kaushal and Sharma (2014) determined the influence of drying process on the osmotically dehydrated jackfruit. Jackfruits (commercial variety) purchased from local market, Sangrur, Punjab were peeled and used for drying. Salt solution of 5, 10, 15 and 20 per cent was used as osmolyte. The osmotically treated samples were dried at 50 °C and were analysed for sensory parameters. Among salt concentrations 15 per cent was considered the best and taken for drying experiments (50, 60 and 70°C) with constant velocity 1.5 m/s, color evaluation and rehydration ratio. Results showed that drying of jackfruit occurred only in the falling rate period: no constant rate period of drying was observed in the increase in drying temperature (50 to 70°C). The highest rehydration ratio (0.43) was observed jackfruit samples dried at 50 °C whereas least (0.40) was observed in those dried at 70 °C. Rehydration ratio (0.42) at 60 °C did not have any significant difference with the sample obtained at 50 °C but was better than the samples obtained at 70 °C. Increase in temperature affected the color of jackfruit samples. The L* values for samples at different drying temperatures varied from 58.699 to 71.185. It was observed that with the increase in temperature from 50 to 70 °C, decrease in L* was observed in all jackfruit samples. Values for a* and b* ranged from 7.553 to 9.404 and 17.144 to 19.383, respectively. On the basis of color, L*, a*, b* values and drying time, the temperature of 60 °C was found to be optimum for dehydration.

Maity *et al.* (2014) observed effect of frying temperatures and durations on the quality of vacuum fried jackfruit chips. Moisture content and breaking force of jackfruit chips decreased with increase in frying temperature and time during vacuum frying whereas the oil content increased. The frying time and temperature tried were 30, 25, and 20 min. at 80, 90, and 100°C, respectively. Jackfruit chips fried at higher temperature resulted in maximum shrinkage (48%). The lightness in terms of Hunter L* value decreased significantly (P<0.05) during frying. Sensory evaluation showed maximum acceptability for jackfruit chips fried at 90°C for 25 min. Frying at lower temperature was found to retain bioactive compounds such as total phenolic, total flavonoids, and total carotenoids.

The effect of pre-treatments on physico-chemical composition of dehydrated jackfruit chips during storage at ambient temperature was investigated by Patil *et al.*, (2014). Five pre-treatments were employed (Blanching, Blanching + 0.5% $CaCl_2$, Blanching + 0.5% Citric acid, Blanching + 0.4% Ascorbic acid). The sample without any pre-treatment served as Control. Storage period studied was of 0, 30 and 60 days. The treatments were evaluated for the impact on chemical composition of chips. Results indicated that moisture, TSS, acidity, reducing sugars, total sugars, non-reducing sugars and β carotene content of dehydrated chips were found maximum in those treated with ascorbic acid, while starch and pH were maximum when treated with $CaCl_2$. Under storage conditions, moisture, TSS, titratable acidity and β carotene increased up to 60 days of storage while reducing sugars, total sugars, non-reducing sugars, starch and pH were decreased significantly. The dehydrated chips of jackfruit pre-treated with ascorbic acid received maximum mean score for overall acceptability (6.91) followed by the treatment (6.20) irrespective of storage period. The organoleptic scores of these dehydrated jackfruit chips declined with increase in storage period.

Ekanayaka *et al.* (2015) aimed to identify and recommend most appropriate pre-treatments for minimal processing of immature jackfruit. Degree of browning, firmness, sensory properties and microbiological quality of minimally processed immature jackfruit were investigated on initial and seventh day after storage at 5–7 °C. Samples were pre-treated with 0.5 and 1 per cent sodium metabisulphite, 1.5 per cent citric acid + 1.5per cent ascorbic acid, 3 per cent citric acid, 3 per cent ascorbic acid and packed in polystyrene packages and over wrapped with polyvinylchloride (PVC) stretch film before storage. When degree of browning in relation to absorbance was assessed, immature jackfruit pre-treated with 1.5 per cent citric acid +1.5 per cent ascorbic acid showed the lowest absorbance at 420 nm and highest reflectance at 450 nm indicating low browning in samples. Variations in firmness were observed after treatment. Microbial counts were within safe-to-consume limits while coliforms were not detected in any of the samples. *Erwiniaphidicola* and *Bacillus subtilis* were identified. Treatments *viz.,* 1.5 per cent citric acid+1.5 per cent ascorbic acid, 1 per cent sodium metabisulphite and 3 per cent citric acid were relatively more successful in retaining acceptable sensory quality of jackfruit even after seven days of storage.

Tender jackfruits were preserved using different methods by Amblily and Davis (2016). The pre-treatments involved, steam blanching with salt and turmeric powder; water blanching with salt, turmeric powder and lime juice and water blanching with turmeric powder and salt. Sun drying, dehydrator and retort machine were used to dry jackfruit. Panel members who were aware about nutrition, between the age group of 20-30 were selected. Microbial analysis was also carried out. Dehydrated tender jackfruit after steam blanching with salt received highest overall acceptability rank (28) followed by the dehydrated jackfruit blanched with salt and turmeric (46.5), while sundried jackfruit after water blanching with salt, lime juice and turmeric powder received lowest rank (130.5). Microbial analysis showed that specific pathogens and total plate count were completely absent in retorted sample of water blanched tender jackfruit with salt, lime juice and turmeric powder.

2.7 Value addition to the jackfruit

Value addition enhances the nutritional quality of food product, it adds new food to the plate. Processing foods for value addition minimises or enhance the loss of nutrients. Fruits and vegetables are mainly seasonal and highly perishable, besides being the treasure trove of nutrients. Hence it is necessary to retain their quality and to keep them available throughout the year. Jackfruit is tasty nutritious as well as locally utilised fruit, but in recent years the importance of the fruit in various stages is recognised and value addition is undertaken.

Hettiaratchi *et al.* (2010) prepared a complete jackfruit breakfast meal and determined the physico-chemical factors of the meal. The test meal comprised of jackfruit flesh (400 g), jack seeds (50 g), coconut scrapings (25 g) and onion (10 g). The composite meal contained 50 g available carbohydrate, 13.5 per cent insoluble dietary fibre, 6.5 per cent soluble dietary fibre and 6.8 per cent protein. The composite meal contained 30 per cent high levels of slowly available glucose and 30.6 percent amylose content. The boiled jackfruit flesh contained disintegrated starch granules while seeds contained both intact swollen and disintegrated granules.

Chakraborty *et al.* (2011) developed jack-passion fruit spread. Jackfruit bulbs were removed from ripe fruit and passed through a pulper fitted with a fine sieve. Passion fruit and jack fruit pulps were mixed at correct ratio with other ingredients, heated at low flame with continuous stirring till the TSS increased between 65 and 68° B, filled into sterilized bottles and stored at ambient (25-37°C) and refrigerated temperature (8-10°C) after capping and labelling. Storage life of jack-passion fruit spread was eight months at ambient temperature (25-37 °C) and 14 months refrigerated temperature (8-10°C). Jack-passion fruit spread scored 3.2 at ambient temperature (25-37 °C) and 3.6 at refrigerated temperature (8-10 °C) on five point hedonic scale. The microbial load of the spread stored under two temperature was slightly lower when stored at refrigerated temperature than at ambient temperature. Yeast load was 6.6 cfu/ml at ambient temperature and 5.7cfu/ml at refrigerated temperature. Bacterial load, was 6.9 cfu/ml at ambient temperature and 4.9 at refrigerated temperature. Nutritional composition of the spread after preparation and at the end of storage at ambient temperature (25-37 °C) showed that initially there was 69.5 per cent °B TSS, 413.2 IU ß-carotene, 1.8 per cent protein, 15.2 mg/100g ascorbic acid, 0.4 per cent titratable acid. At the end of storage at ambient temperature (25-37 ^{0} C), the composition changed to 72.8 per cent total soluble solid, 276.2 IU *β*- carotene, 0.8 per cent protein, 5.1 mg/100g ascorbic acid, 0.6 per cent titratable acid.

Value added fermented jackfruit juice was prepared by Dushyantha *et al.* (2011). Lactobacillus acidophilus was used as source strain which was compared with lactic acid bacteria isolated from perianth, lobes and juice of jackfruit. Soy protein and/or casein was used for value addition. Result showed that pH was highest (3.30) in L. acidophilus fermented juice. Among the strains L acidophilus recorded highest titrable acidity (0.93 %)

maximum residual sugar (2.18 %) and highest protein (3.13%). Among the treatments TSS of treatment with casein and soy protein was 8.8 ^{0}B and was on par with other treatments. Maximum titrable acidity (0.90 %), residual sugar (2.19 %), nitrogen (0.49 %) and protein (3.13%) was recorded in sample treated with casein and soy protein

Patil *et al.* (2011), attempted to develop various products with jackfruit waste from ripe and mature fruit. It included undeveloped perigones rind, core and seeds. The products were developed included jackfruit perigone pickle, jackfruit core and rind pickle, soft and firm flesh jackfruit perigones jelly. The products were evaluated for chemical parameters using standard methods and organoleptically assessed for the colour, flavour and texture at initial, four eight and 12 months of storage employing nine point hedonic scale. Total soluble solids from firm flesh and soft flesh perigone jelly showed gradual increase during storage from initial (68.28 and 68.61^{0}B) to 12 months of storage (70.18 and 71.29^{0}B). On the other hand acidity was found to decline from initial (1.01 and 0.99) to 12 months of storage (0.74 and 0.73) in firm flesh and soft flesh perigone jelly, respectively. pH showed increasing trend from initial (4.64 and 4.66) to 12 months of storage (5.01 and 4.97). The scores for colour, flavour and texture of firm flesh and soft flesh perigone jelly recorded a maximum (6.62, 6.82, 6.77) and (6.69, 6.86, 7.09), respectively when freshly prepared. The scores reduced to 6.48, 6.60, 6.61 in firm flesh jelly and 6.56, 6.69, 6.72, respectively in soft flesh jelly after 12 months of storage. The acidity of firm flesh core pickle was 1.18 per cent initially and increased to 1.60 per cent after 12 months of storage, but the acidity of soft flesh core pickle was 1.14 per cent at initial and increased to 1.64 at 12 months of storage. Further, the acidity of firm flesh and soft flesh perigone pickle was 1.39 and 1.40 per cent, respectively when freshly made and increased to 1.55 and 1.66 per cent, respectively after 12 months of storage. The acidity of firm and soft flesh rind pickle was 1.37 and 1.38 per cent when freshly prepared which increased to 1.67 and 1.69 per cent respectively during 12 months of storage. The pH of firm and soft flesh core pickle was 2.50 and 3.03 respectively when fresh and decreased to 2.05 and 2.03 at 12 months of storage. The pH of firm and soft flesh perigone pickle were 2.52 and 2.53, respectively when freshly made and decreased to 2.17 and 2.07 after 12 months of storage. Overall acceptability scores were 5.74, 7.07 and 5.76 in firm flesh and 5.89, 6.78 and 5.79 in soft flesh core, perigone and rind pickle, respectively, with perigone pickle receiving higher scores than others.

To develop bar from jackfruit seed and pulp, Santos and associates in the year 2011 used ripe jackfruit pulp dried to 20 per cent moisture and seed dried at room temperature. Three formulations of jackfruit and seed incorporated of cereal bars were tested. The cereal bars purchased from market were treated as control. The proportion of dehydrated jackfruit and seed meal were 50:50, 60:40 and 70:30, respectively. Mixture of jackfruit and other ingredients was shaped in aluminium tray, covered with aluminium foil and baked at 110°C for 15mins, further it was cooled and cut into bars. Results showed that among three formulations 60:40 was highly accepted though all the three formulations were acceptable when compared to control. The protein (1.21%) and fiber (1.15%) was higher while carbohydrate (11.35%) and fat (1.56%) were lower in formulated bars when compared to commercially available bars which had 1per cent protein, 19 per cent carbohydrate and 4 per cent fat.

Costa *et al.* (2013) studied addition of dehydrated jackfruit in a probiotic fermented milk. Jackfruit was osmotically (40 % of sucrose and 0.3 % of citric acid) dehydrated and cut, subsequently it was added in stirred probiotic fermented milk. Two formulations were developed, formulation A with dehydrated jackfruit cut into cubes of 0.5 cm and B with dehydrated jackfruit crushed (almost disintegrated). Milk was fermented at 43°C with three strains of lactic acid bacteria: *Bifidobacterium animalis, Lactobacillus acidophilus* and *Streptococcus thermophiles*. The fermentation was stopped when the product reached pH of 4.6 and mixed with 15 per cent dehydrated jackfruit bulbs (w/w). To evaluate the hygienic-sanitary conditions of fermented milk, the enumeration of yeasts and molds, total coliforms and faecal coliforms were done before the sensorial evaluation. The counts of *Bifidobacterium animalis* were 10^{9} CFU/g, whereas other strains had either lower or higher count hence, they were not considered for development of functional food as probiotics. Both formulations showed a high level of acceptance, 82 per cent of the panelists liked the Formulation B (scored the product between grade 9 and 6) and 98 per cent liked the Formulation A (scored the product between grade 9 and 6). The purchase intention was also analysed using a three-point hedonic scale, 78 per cent of the panellists opined to purchase the Formulation A and 48 per cent Formulation B.

Ejiofor and Owuno (2013) analysed proximate composition and sensory properties of jackfruit jam and compared with pineapple jam as a check. Proximate analysis showed that protein content ranged from 0.19-1.12g, vitamin C from 0.0037-0.0099mg/100g, ash from 0.27-1.50g, total acid from 0.054-0.313, pH from 3.35- 5.57 and TSS from 23-70 ^{o}B. Results of sensory evaluation showed that aroma ranged from 3.7-4.4, color ranged from 3.7-4.4, taste from 3.8-4.6, after taste from 3.4-4.3 and general acceptability from 3.9-4.5, on a five point scale with jackfruit jam showing significantly lower values than the control. While texture ranged from 3.7- 4.3 and spreadability from 3.5-4.5 with jackfruit jam having higher values than control.

Jackfruit incorporated high fiber bread was developed utilizing jackfruit rind flour and the physical properties were characterised by Feili *et al.,* (2013). Jackfruit rind flour (JRF) was incorporated into wheat flour (WF) in three different ratios (5, 10 and 15%) respectively. Commercial wheat bread was considered as control. Sensory valuation was conducted for the freshly baked breads by 30 semi-trained panellists. Bread samples which received scores higher than 4 (neither like nor dislike) were considered as acceptable. Increasing the level of JRF caused an increase in hardness and darkness of bread and decrease in volume compared to control. Bread with five per cent JRF had the highest mean scores of overall acceptance (4.03).

Green pickle, rind jelly, bulb jam and jelly, jackfruit and sweet pickle were developed with jackfruit by Mondal and associates in the year 2013. The highest total soluble solids and pH were observed in jelly (65% and 5.04, respectively). Green pickle contained higher amount of vitamin-C (3.44 mg/100 g) and carotenoids (22.78 mg/100 g). Sweet pickle contained the higher amount of moisture (50.95 %). After six months of storage, quality of the processed products regarding color, taste, flavour and texture were similar to that of freshly processed products. After eight to nine months of storage the quality of jam, jelly and squash started to deteriorate but the quality of pickles (both green and sweet-pickle) remained stable even after 12 months of storage.

Fruit juice yoghurt was prepared with the addition of jackfruit juice (Dey *et al.* 2014) at different level (5%, 10% and 15%). The chemical, microbiological and sensory quality characteristics were assessed. Acceptability of the yoghurt decreased with an increase in fruit juice level. Total soluble solid and acidity increased with increase in jackfruit juice incorporation from 33.41 to 36.73 and 0.97 to 1.16 respectively, while protein (4.55% to 4.23%) and fat (7.33% to 6.64%) contents decreased. Experiment showed that total viable count (1.85×10^7 to 1.52×10^7 cfu/ml), total fungal count (1.70×10^4 to 1.01×10^4 cfu/ml) reduced with increase in jackfruit juice.

Hossain *et al.* (2014) developed nutritionally enriched bread with jackfruit seed flour incorporation to wheat flour at the proportion of 25, 35, 45 and 55 per cent. Jackfruit seeds were removed, sliced and pre-treated by blanching with potassium metabisulphite (0.5%) for 10 minutes, dried in cabinet drier at 60^0C for 24 hours. The dried slices were milled into powder. Composite breads with different level of jackfruit seed flour were found to be nutritionally better than control breads. However, there was significant decrease in flavour, color, taste, texture, and overall acceptability of breads with the increase of substitution. The bread with substitution of 25 per cent jackfruit seed flour was most acceptable in terms of nutritional value and overall acceptability compared to the control and other samples.

Totad and co-workers (2014) aimed to develop mixed fruit syrup with ripe sapota, jackfruit and avocado. The fruits were washed, cleaned and cut into small pieces, blended in a mixer and passed through a 30 mesh sieve to remove the fibrous particles and blended at the ratio of 70:25:05. The juice was filtered separately by squeezing through the muslin cloth and mixed in proportion of 45 and 50 per cent with 68 °B, and 70 °B. The Sapota blended with jackfruit and avocado syrup containing 50 per cent juice, 1.50 per cent citric acid and 70 °B was found to be acceptable with good organoleptic scores for appearance (3.71), aroma and flavour (3.91), taste (4.40) and overall acceptability (3.96) on a five point hedonic scale. The syrup bottled in glass bottles, sealed and refrigerated was subjected to organoleptic evaluation after 120 days to assess the quality attributes. Syrup prepared with 50 per cent pulp and 70 °B received higher scores for appearance (3.71), aroma and flavour (3.91), taste (4.40) and overall acceptability (3.96), whereas other formulations score significantly lower on five hedonic scale.

Verma *et al.* (2014) conducted a study to evaluate the substitution of immature jackfruit and chevon in emulsion-based products and to assess their quality during refrigerated storage. Immature jackfruit was substituted at 10, 20, and 30 per cent in the chevon patties and compared with patties from chevon as control. Proximate value showed that ten per cent incorporation had highest moisture (58%), protein (18.39%), fat (11.56%) and ash (2.08%). When stored under refrigerated conditions ($4°C \pm 1°C$) for nine days the patties remained stable with minor changes in physico-chemical characters. Immature jackfruit-based patties recorded hardness in the range of 16.80 to 20.27 N/cm^2 which was significantly lower than control patties (25 N/cm^2). The adhesiveness was in the range of 0.01 ± 0.001 to 0.07 ± 0.007 Ns. However, the springiness did not differ significantly among immature jackfruit incorporated chevon patties. Gumminess was 8.30 ± 0.54, 7.29 ± 0.28 and 7.07 ± 0.16 N/cm^2 respectively for 10, 20 and 30 per cent immature jackfruit incorporation and was significantly lower than the control (14.50 ± 0.42 N/cm^2). The chewiness in patties containing 10, 20 and 30 per cent immature jackfruit was 5.77 ± 0.35, 5.08 ± 0.31 and 4.62 ± 0.16 N/cm which were significantly lower than the control (11.72 ± 0.36 N/cm). pH decreased when stored at 4°C ± 2°C, in all the treatments. Immature jackfruit (30%) incorporated chevon maintained overall acceptability of 6.20 till 9th day whereas others including dropped fall down to 6.16. Overall acceptability score was 6.11 in 20 per cent incorporation which was on par with controlled with score of seven at ninth day of storage.

Veena *et al.* (2015) incorporated raw jackfruit seed and bulb flour in the development of noodles. Composite flour was prepared by mixing refined flour, bulb flour and seed flour in different combinations (40:30:30, 50:25:25, 50:30:20, 50:40:10, 50:10:40, 50:20:30). Noodles were extruded from these combinations and evaluated for sensory parameters. on a five point hedomic scale sensory scores indicated that combinations of 50:10:40 and 50:20:30 were highly accepted with scores of 4.78 and 4.71 for overall acceptability which was on par with control noodles (4.96).

While evaluating the osmotic treatments for production of good quality ripe jackfruit powder, Swami and associates (2016) used sugar solutions of 60, 70 and 80°B. The final product was analysed for chemical (acidity, pH, TSS, reducing Sugar, non-reducing sugar and total sugar) and sensory (texture, colour, flavour and overall acceptability) attributes. Study revealed that the sugar solution of 70°B was best and secured maximum sensory score for colour (7.67), flavour (7.56), texture (7.89), and overall acceptability (7.78). During 12 months of storage, product with 70°B sugar solution stored in met pet poly packaging pouches secured good sensory score for colour (6.50), flavour (6.40), texture (5.71) and overall acceptability (7.30).

Hosamani *et al.* (2016) investigated the effect of partial replacement of wheat flour by different levels of jackfruit powder (25 and 50%) on the color, nutritional and sensory characteristics of the sweet biscuits. Results showed that crude fiber content increased significantly to 0.90 per cent in 50 per cent jackfruit powder incorporated biscuits compared to 0.35 per cent in control biscuits. After storage of three months there was a decrease in reducing, non-reducing and total sugar from 9.57 to 9.0 per cent, 1.68 to 1.47 per cent and 11.25 to 10.47 per cent, respectively in 25 per cent jackfruit powder containing biscuits. Respective reduction in 50 per cent jackfruit powder containing biscuits was 9.30 to 8.98 per cent, 1.20 to 0.99 per cent and 10.5 to 9.67per cent. The moisture content and water activity increased from 4.88 to 5.62 per cent and 0.35 to 0.47 per cent respectively offer storage. Biscuits prepared with 25 per cent of jackfruit powder had higher acceptability scores for sensory characteristics during initial (4.58) and throughout the storage period (4.16).

Fitry and Abas (2018) evaluated the low-fat chicken patties produced by replacing the fat with jackfruit or breadfruit at 50 and 100 per cent. Control patties did not have jackfruit and bread fruit. The samples were analysed for water holding capacity, cooking yield, proximate analysis, colour, texture and sensory parameters. Both bread fruit and jackfruit showed higher value for water holding capacity, moisture and protein compared to the control. Breadfruit and jackfruit at 100 percent replacement had significantly reduced fat of 1.80 per cent and 2.23 per cent, respectively. No significant difference was found between the controls and newly formulated chicken patties with respect to taste. Texture based on the hardness, cohesiveness and chewiness indicate that breadfruit and jackfruit did not affect the texture of patties. Overall acceptability scores for jackfruit replacement was 7.00 and for breadfruit 8.10.

From above reviews, it can be concluded that jackfruit can be successfully used for making chips, wine, sweets, squash, juice, flour etc. It can also be used as whole meal. Young jackfruit curry and pickle were common in northern India whereas matured jackfruits flour or pulp was used widely for making *idli, dosa, upma* etc. in southern India.

2.8 Utilization of fruit for development of composite flour

Composite flour was developed for *missi roti* and valuated by Kadam and co-workers (2012), using wheat flour, chickpea, soybean and *methi* leaves powder. Four types of blends were tried. A- wheat flour: chickpea flour (80:20). B- wheat flour: full fat soy flour (90:10) C- wheat flour: chickpea flour: soy flour (80:10:10) and D- wheat flour: chickpea flour: soy flour: *methi* leaves powder (75: 10: 10: 05). The fat content ranged from 1.53 to 3.45 per cent, fibre 1.24 to 2.05 per cent, protein 11.8 to 15.37per cent, ash 2.08 to 2.7 per cent and carbohydrates ranged from 65.99 to 74.2 per cent. Iron was high in *methi* supplemented blend. All these blended flours were found to have good sensory quality with score of seven or above for overall acceptability. All these blended flours could be stored in tin boxes or polyethylene bags for the period of three months without any deterioration of quality. The supplementation of five per cent *methi* leaves powder increased the nutritional quality of flour particularly the minerals (iron and calcium) and fibres.

Menon *et al.* (2014) studied the feasibility of utilizing composite flour of cereal-legume-seed kernel in the preparation of bread. The composite flour was prepared using refined wheat flour (WF), sprouted mung bean flour (MF), soy flour (SF) and mango kernel flour (MKF). Three variations of composite flour were used for preparation of experimental breads. Combination of V-I WF: MF: SF: MKF used were V-II 70:10:10:10 and V-III 60:14:13:13. Refined wheat flour bread served as control. Pertinent physico-chemical, functional and organoleptic attributes were studied in composite flours and respective bread. Baking losses were estimated in experimental breads. Physical characteristics of the bread revealed a decrease in loaf weight (1.25 %), height (14 %) and volume (25 %) with subsequent increase in mango kernel flour. V-1 had lower non significant score of 7.23±0.86 for overall acceptability when compared with the control (7.5±0.5), whereas, V-II and V-III received significantly lower scores than control because of bitterness in the product.

Ahmed and Uoorj (2015) formulated composite flours using wheat flour, psyllium, oats and barley at two different levels (75:5:10:10 and 60:10:15:15). *Rotis* were prepared from all formulations and evaluated for organoleptic various starch fractions were analysed using controlled enzymatic digestion. The digestibility characteristics were studied using amylolysis kinetics employing porcine pancreatic α-amylase in vitro. Results showed that both the variations had acceptable sensory scores of 8.5 and 7.8. The formulations had significantly lower values for total starch (33.83 and 28.19 %), rapidly digestible starch (5.22 and 4.37%), resistant starch (22.69 and 8.955%), starch digestibility index (14.76 and 16.71%), rapidly available glucose (7.82 and 7.72%) than those reported in control (39.85, 26.91, 19.50 and 9.96% respectively). Between the two variations, first formulation showed better starch digestibility characteristics with significantly lower starch digestibility index. In case of amylolysis kinetics, both the variations significantly inhibited α-amylase as reflected by lower glucose diffusion and significantly higher glucose dialysis retardation index compared to control.

Orange fleshed sweet potato flour was blended with wheat flour to produce composite flour breads (Dako *et al.,* 2016). Six blending ratios of sweet potato flour with wheat flour (0:100, 5:95, 10:90, 15:85, 20:80 and 25:75) were tried. Functional properties of composite flour such as wet gluten decreased and water absorption capacity increased with an increase in sweet potato flour. Quality parameters of breads such as volume (467.98 to 260.09cm^3), specific volume (5.68 to 2.75 cm^3/g) and height (5.77 to 3.75cm) decreased significantly but loaf weight increased from 84.01 to 94.78 g, as the ratio of sweet potato flour increased. Increase of sweet potato flour significantly increased the moisture (30.77 -37.13 %), ash (1.95 to 2.83%), fiber (1.76 to 2.75%), carbohydrate (83.74 to 84.85%), calcium (21.08 to 31.42mg/100gm), iron(2.92 to 5.09mg/100gm) and zinc (0.52 to 0.68mg/100gm) content of the breads and resulted in a decrease in the fat (1.76 to 2.75%), protein(11.17 to 8.34%), energy (395 to 384 kcal), phosphorus (19.23-17.51mg/100gm), phytate (98.88 to 67.43mg/100gm), phytate: iron (2.89 to 1.13 mg/100gm), phytate: calcium(0.29 to 0.14mg/100gm), phytate: zinc (18.82 to 10.25mg/100gm)and [phytate x calcium]: zinc(0.099 t0 0.081mg/100gm). Sensory attributes such as appearance (7.92), aroma (7.58), taste (7.46), mouth feel (7.08) and overall acceptability (7.17) indicated that control bread was more preferred by consumers than composite flour breads. However, breads prepared with 15 per cent sweet potato flour was accepted by consumers (appearance-6.08, aroma-6.25, taste-6.65, mouth feel-5.45 and overall acceptability -6.17).

Physico-chemical and functional properties of sweet potato-wheat composite flour and sensory attributes of doughnuts, bread, chips and biscuits were studied by Tortoe *et al.* (2016). Moisture content of sweet potato flour was significantly lower than wheat flour and sweet potato-wheat composite flours (5%, 10%, 15%, 20%, and 30%). The sweet potato flour had 89.2 per cent carbohydrate and 379 kcal of energy per 100 g. The pH of sweet potato flour was significantly lower, compared to wheat flour. Emulsion capacity was higher (52.4%) for sweet potato flour than wheat flour (48.4%). Pasting temperatures were similar for the flours but duration differed. Best overall acceptability scores was found in 15 per cent blend for doughnuts (7.0), bread (7.5), chips (7.6), and biscuits (7.9). Moisture decreases with increase in sweet potato flour from (12.83 to 1089%). Decrease in pH was recorded with increase in sweet potato flour per cent from 6.18 to 5.79. Bulk density increases (0.79 to o.82), emulsification capacity increases from 46.7 to 52.2 with increases sweet potato flour. Product developed from composite flour like doughnut obtained 7.8 overall acceptability at 5 per cent, chips scored 7.7 overall acceptability at 10 and 20 per cent, bread and biscuit scored 8.1 and 8.3 overall acceptability at five per cent sweet potato flour incorporation.

Composite flours are nutritionally advantageous than sole flour. Composite flour shows good potential for use as a functional agent in bakery products and can be an ideal partner in managing various life style disorders like diabetes, cardio vascular diseases, celiac diseases etc.

2.9 Storage quality of fruit, vegetable and cereal based composite flour

Storage of flours is an important indicator of later usage as well as market stability of the product. The packaging material, storage conditions and period of storage influences the quality of the product.

Singh *et al.* (2011) formulated two millet–wheat composite flours, CF1 and CF2, based on the rheological and textural properties of dough. The optimized contents of composite flour CF1 were, 31.4 per cent wheat flour, 61.8 per cent barnyard millet flour and 6.8 per cent gluten. The optimized components of the composite flour CF2 were 70.6 % wheat flour, 9.1 % barnyard millet flour, 10.2 % proso millet flour and 10.1 % finger millet flour. Millet–wheat composite flours were stored in three different packaging materials, [(high-density polyethylene (HDPE), low-density polyethylene (LDPE), and metallized polyester (MP)], at 90 per cent RH and 40 °C for 90 days. Moisture gain in CF1 was minimum (55%) when packed in MP as compared with LDPE (124%) and HDPE (100%) after 90 days of storage. The shelf lives of the composite flours were estimated based on their critical moisture contents. After 90 days of storage CF1, registered highest retention of starch (91.85%) when packed in MP followed by HDPE (87.5%) and LDPE (84.8%). However, the retention was not significant in CF2 when packed in all three packaging materials. After 90 days of storage, the predicted shelf life of CF1 and CF2 in LDPE, HDPE, and MP packaging materials were 30, 38, and 61 days and 26, 34, and 54 days, respectively.

Kadam *et al.* (2012) evaluated shelf-life of composite flours prepared with wheat flour, chickpea, soybean and *methi* leaves powder in terms of moisture and fatty acid acidity.

During storage moisture varied from 8.4 to 10.28 per cent. The average values of moisture in different flours were 8.66, 9.18, 9.81, and 10.10 per cent on 0, 30, 60, and 90 days respectively. The variations in moisture content did not vary significantly. On storage of flours, the values of fatty acid acidity were lower in polyethylene bags (0.152-0.132) compared to tin boxes (0.161-0.270).

Shobha *et al.* (2015) tried eight types of composite flour for noodle preparation by blending varied amount of maize flour, refined wheat flour, rice flour, wheat gluten, soya protein isolate, kansui (Sodium carbonates), and potato starch. The flours were evaluated for storage quality. There was no significant increase in moisture and peroxide values up to three months of storage. The overall acceptability scores were 4.0, 4.1, & 4.2 respectively for normal noodle, quality protein maize noodle and control noodle. However the noodles were within the acceptable range up to six months of storage with an overall acceptability score of 3.0, 3.4 and 3.2 for normal noodle, quality protein maize noodle and control noodle, respectively on a five point hedonic scale.

Rathod *et al.* (2019) carried out research to know the storage quality of high fiber composite flour. The blends were prepared by mixing wheat with foxtail millet, little millet and finger millet, fenugreek seeds (1 g) and roasted soy bean (10 g) at various levels to provide at least 12-15 g of fibre. The millet composite flour was packed and sealed in two different packaging materials (high density poly ethylene and metalized polypropylene) for storage at ambient temperature (20.80 to 31.18 °C) and RH of (36.83 to 80.91%). The moisture content of flour packed in Metalized Poly Propylene (MPP) packaging material was 7.07 per cent initially and increased significantly after 75 days of storage (7.57%), and further increased to 7.63 per cent after 150 days of storage. Free fatty acid was initially 0.12 mg/KOH/g and increased significantly to 0.30 mg/KOH/g after 90 days when packed in HDPE. In the Metalized Poly Propylene (MPP) the free fatty acid content of composite flour increased to 0.18 mg/KOH/g at 45 days of storage and significant increase was seen after 90, 120, 150 and 180 days of storage.

Studies of storage quality represent that shelf life of flours is enhanced with the help of different packaging material. Good selection of storage conditions and packaging material helped in retaining the chemical as well as physical quality of flours.

2.10 Glycemic effect of composite flour

The GI is originally meant to be an index of the blood glucose raising potential of the available carbohydrate in foods. Glycemic index (GI) is the measure of immediate effect on blood glucose level after consumption of food. It is expressed as percentage of incremental area under the curve (iAUC) of a test food with source to a standard food (white bread or glucose) containing the same amount of available carbohydrates.

Radhika *et al.* (2010) compared the glycaemic index (GI) of newly developed '*atta* mix' *roti* with whole wheat flour *roti*. Eighteen healthy non-diabetic subjects consumed 50 g available carbohydrate portions of a source food (glucose) and two test foods (whole wheat flour *roti* and *atta* mix *roti*) in random order after an overnight fast. Capillary blood samples were measured from finger-prick samples in fasted 25 subjects at 0, 15, 30, 45, 60, 90 and 120 min after consumption of food from the start of each food. No significant difference was observed between *roti* prepared from whole wheat flour and *atta* mix in terms of appearance, texture, flavour, taste or overall acceptability. For each test food, the incremental area under the curve and GI values were determined. The GI of *atta* mix *roti* (27·3) was considerably lower than the whole wheat roti (45·1).

The glycemic index of meals prepared using cocoyam with plantain and cowpea flour blend was determined by Akinlotan *et al.* (2015). Three ratios, namely 95/5, 75/25 and 50/50 each were produced from differently processed cocoyam/plantain and cocoyam/cowpea flour respectively. A total of thirty (30) healthy volunteers were recruited by random sampling and further divided into ten (10) volunteers each. Pre-tested structured questionnaire was used to collected information on the clinical and anthropometric data. Blood samples were taken from the finger tips by pricking. Majority of subjects were within the age range of 20-39 years, the mean body mass index of 25.24 kg/m². The mean fasting blood sugar was 73.11mmol/L. The ratio of 50:50 cocoyam-cowpea blend had medium GI of 60, 61 and 58 for sun dried, drum dried and oven dried respectively, while sun dried and drum dried cocoyam - plantain blends in the ratio of 50:50 had low GI of 59 and 58.

Verma *et al.* (2017) aimed to determine the glycemic index of the developed ready to eat functional food products made from composite flour. Composite flour was formulated using wheat flour, barley flour, garlic powder and black cumin seed in different combinations. Best acceptable combination (wheat flour- 50%, barley flour-37%, garlic powder-10% and black cumin seed- 3%) was used to develop *mathri* and biscuit. Normal subjects (10) aged between 20 to 25 years were selected. They were clinically normal and non-diabetic. Study revealed that composite flour based *mathri* had low glycemic index (54.48) while control *mathri* had high glycemic index (73.91). Composite flour based biscuits had moderate glycemic index (56.69) while control biscuits had high glycemic index (83.05). Study concluded that glycemic index of the product *mathri* and biscuits prepared from composite flour to have glycemic index of 54.48 and 56.69 which can be grouped as low glycemic and moderate glycemic index foods respectively.

Studies have shown that with the help of composite flour GI can be lowered by blending novel underutilized flour from different sources in to most commonly used flours like rice or wheat.

CHAPTER -3
MATERIAL AND METHODS

Jackfruit is universally consumed fruit, which is also known as poor man's fruit and it is edible from 20th day of genesis till ripening. Although it is rich in nutrients and full of therapeutic qualities it is not much popular among the population except few pockets of growers. Thus, the present study entitled "Value addition, and therapeutic significance of jackfruit (*Artocarpus Heterophyllus*)" was conducted in the department of Food Science and Nutrition, College of Community Science, UAS Dharwad. Keeping the objectives in mind methodology was sketched. The material use and methodology adopted for the research is narrated in this chapter under the following sub heads;

3.1. Collection of information about jackfruit

3.2. Procurement of material

3.3. Physical properties of whole fruit at different stages of maturity

3.4. Preparation of jackfruit for chemical analysis

3.5. Proximate analysis and mineral composition of the jackfruit at different stages of maturity

3.6. Carbohydrate profile of jackfruit at different stages of maturity

3.7. Nutritional quality of jackfruit at different stages of maturity

3.8. Antioxidant components and activity of jackfruit at different stages of maturity

3.9. Antidiabetic property of jackfruit at different stages of maturity

3.10. Value addition to jackfruit

3.11. Storage quality of developed antidiabetic composite mix

3.12. Efficacy of the developed antidiabetic mix in controlling blood glucose

3.13. Acceptability of developed product among diabetic population

3.14. Cost analysis of developed composite flour mix

3.15 Statistical analysis

Detailed research design is indicated in Fig 1.

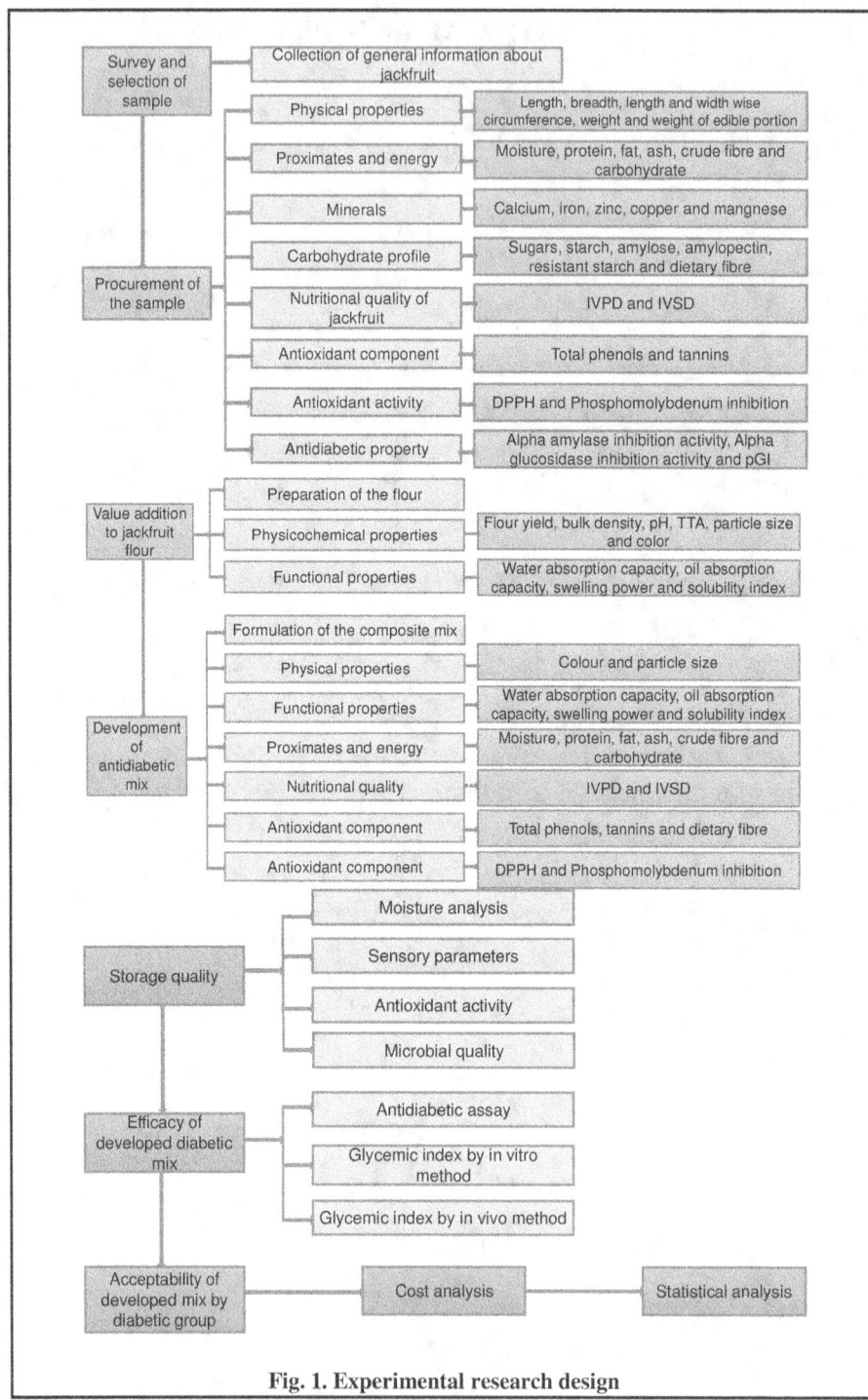

Fig. 1. Experimental research design

3.1 COLLECTION OF INFORMATION ABOUT JACKFRUIT

A simple survey was conducted in Sirsi district of Karnataka (Plate 1) where jackfruit is grown abundantly, by visiting 25 families. Information was collected on utilization, preparations, method of consumption, storage methods and also the knowledge regarding therapeutic properties of jackfruit.

3.2 PROCUREMENT OF MATERIAL

3.2.1. Fruits and other ingredients

Initially ten Jackfruits at every three different stages of maturity were procured from specific trees situated on Dharwad campus of University of Agricultural Sciences and nearby areas of Dharwad, Karnataka, during months of January to June (Plate 2). Horticulturists were consulted to understand the maturity at different stages of growth. Other ingredients like wheat flour, spices and condiments were procured from local market of Dharwad for the value addition. Samples were processed and stored for further study.

3.2.2. Procurement of chemicals

All chemicals used for analysis were of analytical grade. 2, 2-diphenyl-1-picrylhydrazyl (DPPH), Gallic acid and Folin Ciocalteu Reagent (FCR) were of Hi-media. Pepsin NF and pancreatin 4 x NF used in the study were of Loba make. Termamyl 120 L and amylose from potato starch, alpha-amylase and alpha-glucosidase were purchased from Sigma-Aldrich Chemical Co. etc.

3.3. PHYSICAL PROPERTIES OF WHOLE FRUIT AT DIFFERENT STAGES OF MATURITY

The whole fruits were used for measuring physical properties such as weight, length, breadth, lengthwise circumference, width wise circumference, weight of edible portion and weight of seed. Ten fruits each, at different stages of maturity were selected randomly.

3.3.1. Length and breadth of the fruit

Length of ten selected jackfruits were obtained by placing the fruit lengthwise on paper and the ends marked. The measurements were recorded in centimetre using a scale and average was calculated.

Plate 1. Collecting information about jackfruit and its utilization in Sirsi, Karnataka

Plate 2. Procurement of jackfruit

Breadth of the jackfruit was obtained by placing ten selected fruits breadth wise on a paper and the ends marked. The measurements of breadth were recorded using a scale and average calculated in centimetre.

3.3.2. Length wise and width wise circumference of fruit

Length wise circumference of the ten selected fruits was measured by passing flexible non stretchable tape around the central part of the fruit along the length. Measurement was expressed in centimetre.

Width wise circumference of the ten selected fruits was measured by passing flexible non stretchable tape around upper, middle and lower part of the fruit along the breadth. The average of three measurements for each fruit was calculated and expressed in centimetre.

3.3.3. Weight

Ten individual fruits of each stage of maturity were selected randomly and weighed using the digitalized weighing balance, average was calculated and expressed in kilo grams (kg).

3.3.4. Weight of edible portion of fruit

In case of immature stage, peel was removed and edible portion was weighed. For matured and ripe fruits, selected ten fruits were cut open and bulbs, seeds, rinds, rags and core separated. Using digital weighing balance the bulbs were weighed as edible part and expressed in kilograms per fruit. The seeds were weighed separately, average calculated and expressed in kilogram per fruit

3.4. PREPARATION OF JACKFRUIT FOR CHEMICAL ANALYSIS

The immature, mature and ripe fruits (ten each) were cut, bulbs separated from inedible parts and seeds were removed for mature and ripe fruits. The bulbs were dried in hot air oven at 45-50 $^{\circ}$C till crisp (Fig 2).

3.5. PROXIMATE ANALYSIS AND MINERAL COMPOSITION OF THE JACKFRUIT AT DIFFERENT STAGES OF MATURITY

Proximate composition and macro and micro minerals were analysed in jackfruit powder.

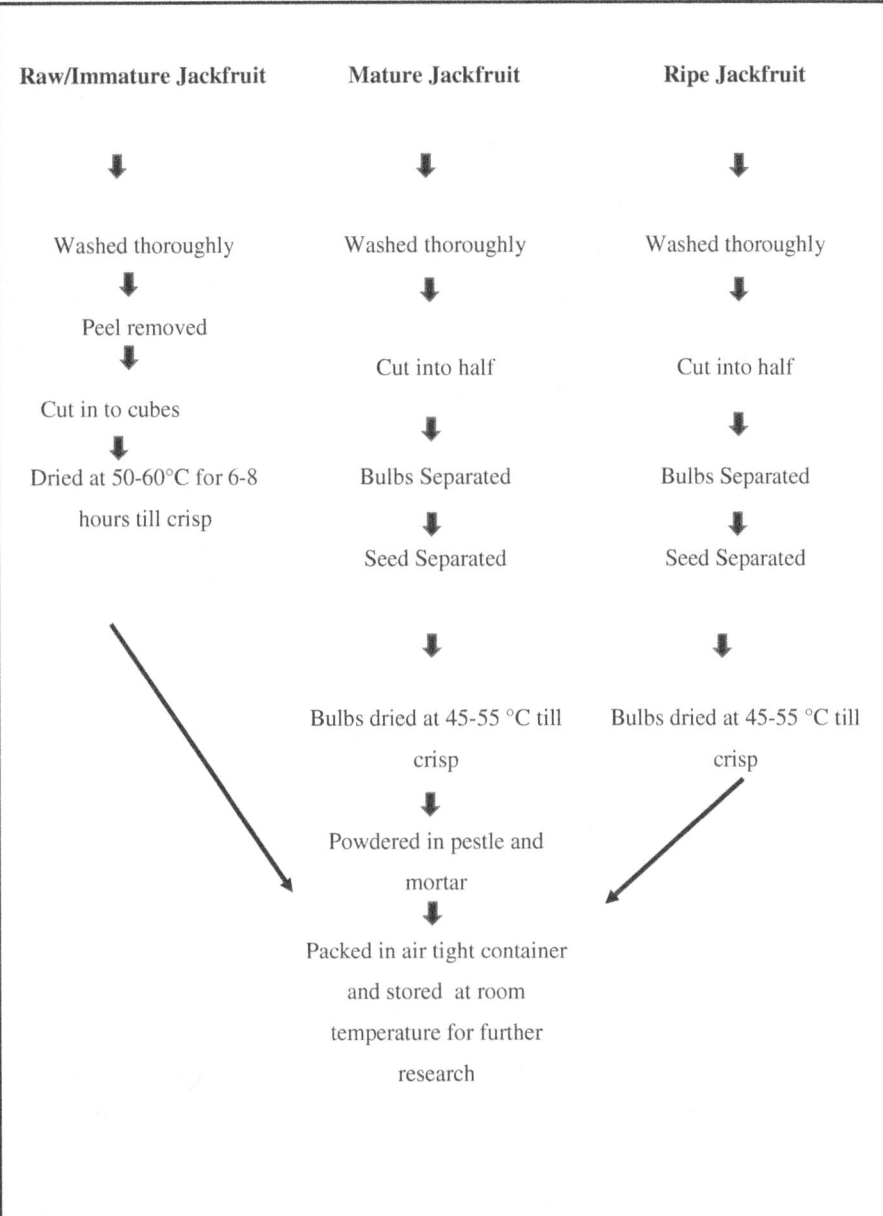

Raw/Immature Jackfruit

⬇

Washed thoroughly
⬇
Peel removed
⬇
Cut in to cubes
⬇
Dried at 50-60°C for 6-8

hours till crisp

Mature Jackfruit

⬇

Washed thoroughly
⬇

Cut into half

⬇

Bulbs Separated
⬇

Seed Separated

⬇

Bulbs dried at 45-55 °C till

crisp
⬇

Powdered in pestle and

mortar
⬇

Packed in air tight container

and stored at room

temperature for further

research

Ripe Jackfruit

⬇

Washed thoroughly
⬇

Cut into half

⬇

Bulbs Separated
⬇

Seed Separated

⬇

Bulbs dried at 45-55 °C till

crisp

Fig. 2. Flow chart of jackfruit preparation for chemical analysis

3.5.1 Proximate composition

Compounds occurring naturally in animal and vegetable tissues, the proximate principles are moisture, proteins, fats, fiber carbohydrates and total minerals.

3.5.1.1. Estimation of moisture

Moisture was determined by weighing accurately about ten grams of powdered sample in a moisture cup and dried in an oven at 105 °C till the weight of the moisture cup with its contents was constant. Each time before weighing, the moisture cup was cooled in desiccator. Moisture content of the sample was expressed as g/100g of sample (Anon, 2019).

$$Moisture\ content\ (\%) = \frac{Initial\ weight\ of\ the\ sample\ (g) - Final\ weight\ weight\ of\ the\ sample\ (g)}{Weight\ of\ the\ sample\ (g)} \times 100$$

3.5.1.2 Estimation of crude Fat

Fat was estimated as crude ether extract of the dry material. The moisture free sample (5g) was weighed accurately into a thimble and plugged with cotton. The thimble was then placed in a Soxhlet apparatus (pelican socsplus) and extracted with anhydrous ether (60-80°C) for about three hours. Ether was then evaporated and the beaker with the residue dried in an oven at 60 to 80 °C, cooled in a desiccator and weighed (Anon, 2000).

$$Fat\ content\ (g\ /\ 100g) = \frac{Weight\ of\ ether\ extract\ (g)}{Weight\ of\ the\ sample} \times 100$$

3.5.1.3 Estimation of Protein

The protein content of the dried sample was estimated as per cent total nitrogen by the Micro-kjeldahl method (Anon, 2019) and computed by multiplying the per cent nitrogen with conversion factor 6.25.

Organic nitrogen present in food sample was digested by heating with sulfuric acid in the presence of catalyst. The organic nitrogen was converted to ammonium sulphate. Ammonia was liberated by making the solution alkaline, which was trapped in boric acid to form ammonium borate. Nitrogen content was then estimated by titration with standard hydrochloric acid, using a mixed indicator.

For the digestion of samples, Kelplus-Classic Dx (Pelican equipments) digestion unit was used. The distillation was carried out in Kelplus- Classic Dx (Pelican equipments) automatically.

$$Protein\ (\%) = \frac{(Titrate - blank) \times Normality\ of\ HCl \times 14.007 \times 6.25}{Sample\ weight\ (g)} \times 100$$

3.5.1.4 Estimation of crude fibre

Moisture and fat free sample was hydrolysed with acid (1.25% H_2SO_4) and subsequently with alkali (1.25% NaOH) and the residue obtained after final filtration was weighed, incinerated, cooled and weighed again. The loss in weight was considered as the crude fibre content (Anon 2000).

$$Crude\ fibre\ (g/100g) = \frac{(We - Wa)}{Weight\ of\ moisture\ and\ fat\ free\ sample} \times 100$$

Where,

We – Weight of residue with crucible

Wa – Weight of the ash with crucible

3.5.1.5 Estimation of ash

Total mineral content (ash) was estimated by taking about five grams of moisture and fat free sample into a silica crucible (which has previously been heated to about 600 °C and cooled). The crucible was placed on a clay pipe triangle and heated over a low flame for decarbonisation followed by heating in a muffle furnace for about four to five hours at 600 °C. It was then cooled in a desicator and weighed. This was repeated till two consecutive weights were same and the ash was almost white or greyish white in color.

$$Ash\ content\ (g/100g) = \frac{W1 - W2}{Weight\ of\ the\ sample} \times 100$$

Where, W1-weight of crucible with sample

W2-weight of crucible after ashing

3.5.1.6 Carbohydrate by difference method

The carbohydrate content was calculated by difference method i.e. deducting the sum of the values for moisture, crude protein, crude fat and ash from 100 for total carbohydrate and by deducting the sum of the values for moisture, crude protein, crude fat, ash and dietary fiber from 100 for available carbohydrate (FAO, 1998)

$Available\ Carbohydrate\ (g/100g)$
$$= 100 - [Moisture\ (g) + Fat\ (g) + Protein + Dietary\ fibre\ (g) + Ash\ (g)]$$

$Total\ Carbohydrate\ (g/100g)$
$$= 100 - [Moisture\ (g) + Fat\ (g) + Protein\ (g) + Ash\ (g)]$$

3.5.2 Physiological energy

The calorific value of the sample was computed by multiplying the values of carbohydrate, protein and fat with respective Atwater values (4, 4 and 9) and summing-up

$$Total\ energy\ (Kcal/100g) = [(\%carbohydrate \times 4) + (\%protein \times 4) + (\%fat \times 9)]$$

3.5.3 Mineral composition of jackfruit at different stages of maturity

Minerals are inorganic substances required by the body in small amounts for a variety of functions. Maturity and advancement towards ripening are known to affect concentration of minerals in food. Hence, macro minerals like calcium and micro minerals like iron, zinc, copper and manganese in jackfruit at different stages of maturity were analysed.

3.5.3.1. Macro mineral

Macro minerals are present in more than 5 per cent of body weight in human beings. Macro minerals include calcium, chlorine, magnesium, phosphorus, potassium, sodium, and sulphur.

Estimation of calcium was carried out by titrimetric method (Oser, 1965). Calcium was precipitated as calcium oxalate. The precipitate was dissolved in hot dilute sulphuric acid and titrated against standard potassium permanganate.

3.5.3.2. Micro minerals

The trace elements (iron, zinc, copper and manganese) were estimated using Atomic Absorption Spectrophotometry. The sample was subjected to wet digestion using triacid mixture (Anon., 2000). A known aliquot of test sample was suitably diluted and micronutrients in the test sample (Cu, Mn, Zn and Fe) were determined using Atomic Absorption Spectrophotometer (model: AAS GBS Avanta). Calibration of measurements was performed using commercial standards.

3.6 CARBOHYDRATE PROFILE OF JACKFRUIT AT DIFFERENT STAGES OF MATURITY

Carbohydrates constitute storage form of energy and play an important role in food preparation as a functional ingredient. Carbohydrate profile includes total, reducing and non-reducing sugars, total starch, amylose and amylopectin. The profile was analysed using standard methods as detailed below;

3.6.1 Sugars

The total and reducing sugars was estimated by Nelson- Somogyi's method with modifications indicated by Ranganna (1986). Sugars contain free aldehyde or keto groups, hence, when heated with alkaline copper tartrate reduce the copper from cupric to cuprous state resulting in the formation of cuprous oxide. When cuprous oxide was treated with arsenomolybdic acid, the reduction of molybdic acid to molybdenum results in blue coloration. Non- reducing sugars was computed by subtracting reducing sugars from total sugars and multiplying with 0.95 a constant conversion factor.

Non- reducing sugars = [Total sugars - Reducing sugars] × 0.95

3.6.2 Starch

Sample was repeatedly treated with hot 80 per cent alcohol. The residue rich in starch was solubilised with perchloric acid and filtered. Extract was treated with anthrone sulphuric acid to determine glucose. Glucose value was multiplied by 0.9 to convert into starch (McCready *et al.*, 1950).

3.6.3 Amylose and amylopectin Total amylose was estimated by following the method of Soubhagya and Bhattacharya (1979). One hundred mg of sample was weighed accurately and taken in a 100 ml volumetric flask. One ml of alcohol was added and mixed well followed by 10 ml of 1 N NaOH, left overnight. Next day the volume was made up to 100 ml with distilled water mixed thoroughly. Five ml aliquot was taken into a 100 ml volumetric flask, three drops of

phenolphthalein indicator and 50 ml of distilled water was added, which turned pink. Then 0.1 N HCl, was added till it turned colourless. To this, 2 ml of 0.2 per cent iodine solution was added and volume was made up to 100 ml with boiled distilled water. The purple-blue color was read at 600 nm. Amylopectin content was derived after subtracting amylose from total starch content.

3.6.4 Resistant starch (RS) (McCleary and Monaghan, 2002)

Resistant starch was determined using kit (K-RSTAR, Megazyme Bray, Co. Wicklow, Ireland). Defatted and milled sample (100±0.5mg) was incubated with pancreatic α-amylase (10 mg/ml) solution containing amyloglucosidase for 16 h at $37^{\circ}C$ with constant shaking. After hydrolysis, samples were washed thrice with 50 per cent ethanol. The pellet separated from supernatant at 1,500 rpm for 10 min in centrifuge was further digested with 2M KOH. Digested pellet and supernatantwere separately incubated with amyloglucosidase. Glucose released was measured using a glucose oxidase-peroxidase (GOPOD) reagent kit (K-GLOX, Megazyme Bray, Co. Wicklow, Ireland) by recording absorbance at 510 nm against the reagent blank. The glucose content of the supernatant and digested pellet were used for calculation of resistant starch by applying the factor of 0.9.

$$Resistant\ Starch\ (\%\ ) = ABS \times F \times \frac{10.3}{0.1} \times \frac{1}{1000} \times \frac{100}{w} \times \frac{162}{180}$$

= ABS x F/W x 9.27

Where ,

ABS is absorbance , F is obtained by dividing the amount of D-glucose by absorbance obtained for this amount in standard assay and W is weight of the sample.

162/180 = factor to convert from free D-glucose

3.6.5 Dietary fibre

Soluble, insoluble and total components of dietary fibre were estimated using amyloglucosidase (Asp *et al.*, 1983). Dietary fiber content in a sample was measured using an enzymatic-gravimetric method. Defatted sample was treated with enzymes that stimulate the digestive process in the human small intestine. Digestible carbohydrates were broken down into simple sugars and removed from the sample by precipitation and filtration. Non-digestible precipitate contained the dietary fiber along with protein and inorganic material.

Thus, to obtain the amount of dietary fiber present, the sample was incinerated at 550 °C for at least five hrs, cooled in desiccator and weighed.

3.7 NUTRITIONAL QUALITY OF JACKFRUIT AT DIFFERENT STAGES OF MATURITY

Scientific evidence of human digestion of foods gathered during the last decades has strengthened the relationship between digestibility and the possible effects of foods on human health. The high complexity of the gastrointestinal environment and the lack of an easy direct access to most of the parts of the gastrointestinal tract with the exception of the oral cavity, prevent the broad implementation of *in vivo* animal, or human trials for assessing the digestion, absorption, and metabolism of dietary food ingredients. Hence, *in vitro* testing of quality was conducted using jackfruit at different levels of maturity.

3.7.1 *in-vitro* protein digestibility (IVPD)

In-vitro protein digestibility was studied using method described by Moulishwar *et al.* (1993). Slurried sample containing 100 mg of protein was treated with 0.1 N HCL containing 12.5 mg of pepsin (1:2500) at 37 °C in shaker water bath for three hours. Digested sample was neutralized with 0.5 N NaOH, then 25 ml of phosphate buffer containing six mg of pancreatin was added and incubated for 24 hours at 37 °C in incubation chamber. The volume was made upto 100 ml with distilled water and 50 ml of the aliquot was treated with 10 per cent trichloroacetic acid and left overnight to precipitate the proteins. The suspensions were centrifuged at 6000 rpm for 20 min and residue was analysed for protein by microkjeldahl method (Kelplus-Pelican). The amount of protein digested was calculated as

$$\text{Digested protein } (\%) = \frac{\text{Total protein} - \text{Undigested protein}}{\text{Total protein}} \times 100$$

3.7.2 *in-vitro* starch digestibility (IVSD)

In-vitro method of Odenigbo *et al.*(2012) based on the modified procedure of Goñi *et al.*(1997) was used to assess the *in-vitro* starch digestibility. Sample (0.5 mg) was incubated with 10 ml HCl–KCl buffer (pH 1.5) and 20 mg pepsin at 40°C for one hour with constant shaking. The pH was raised with the addition of 200 µl pancreatic α-amylase solution (1.5 mg /10 ml phosphate buffer) and incubated at 37°C for 45 min. The enzyme reaction was stopped with 70 µl Na$_2$CO$_3$ solution and samples diluted to 25 ml with tris-maleate buffer (pH 6.9).

Five ml of pancreatic α-amylase solution (1mg /5 ml tris-maleate buffer) was then added to the sample and incubated at 37°C with constant shaking. Aliquots (triplicates) of one ml were drawn at 30, 90, and 120 min and placed in boiling water bath with vigorous shaking for five minute to stop the enzyme reaction. The samples were further refrigerated (4°C) until the end of incubation time (120 min). Aliquots were treated with three ml of 0.4 M sodium acetate buffer (pH 4.75) and 60 μl of amyloglucosidase (3,300 U/ml) incubated at 60°C for 45 min with constant shaking as described in Nelson Somogy's method (Ranganna, 1986). Further readings were taken at 30, 90 and 120 min at 620 nm in bio-spectrophotometer.

The 30 min and 120 min hydrolysis represented the rapidly digestible starch (RDS) and slowly digestible starch (SDS) respectively (Rosin *et al.*, 2002). Starch digestibility index (SDI) was calculated using the equation SDI = RDS/Total starch × 100 (Rashmi and Urooj, 2003).

Glucose was used as standard and degree of hydrolysis was expressed as milligrams of glucose liberated from food after correction for blank values. Starch equivalent was calculated by multiplying the obtained value with 0.9 (Moulishwar *et al.*, 1993).

3.8 ANTIOXIDANT COMPONENTS AND ACTIVITY OF JACKFRUIT AT DIFFERENT STAGES OF MATURITY

Any molecule which reduces damage due to oxygen caused by free radicals are called as antioxidants. Diet high in antioxidants may reduce the risk of many diseases, including heart disease, certain cancers, skin infections, diabetes etc. Antioxidants are capable of stabilizing, or deactivating free radicals before they attack cells. Antioxidants are absolutely critical for maintaining optimal cellular and systemic health and well-being. There are various types of antioxidants like dietary, metal binding, endogenous antioxidants and phytonutrients.

3.8.1 Antioxidant components of jackfruit at different stages of maturity

Total phenols, an important class of secondary metabolites, consist of structurally heterogeneous group ranging from simple phenolic acids to complex polymeric structure which acts as antioxidant when consumed for longer period of time. Tannin, a polyphenol shows strong antioxidant activity because of abundance of hydroxyl group present in it. Antioxidant dietary fiber is proposed as a new potential antioxidant ingredient which proved to prevent or delay lipid oxidation in foods and also known to bring changes in sensory characteristics of food product.

3.8.1.1 Total Phenols

Extraction of powdered and defatted samples was carried out using 80 per cent ethanol. Supernatant was evaporated and used for estimation. Total phenol estimation was carried out with the Folin-Ciocalteau Reagent. Phenols react with phosphomolybdic acid in Folin-Ciocalteau reagent in alkaline medium and produce blue (molybdenum blue) coloured complex. The absorbance of samples was read at 650 nm. Gallic acid was used as the standard and results were expressed as gallic acid equivalent (Ercisli, and Orhan, 2008).

3.8.1.2 Tannins

Powdered and defatted sample extracts were prepared using 85 per cent methanol containing one percent sulphuric acid and allowed to stand for 30 min with occasional shaking. Extract was filtered using Whatman no. 1 filter paper and filterate was used for estimation. Tannins were estimated calorimetrically, based on the measurement of blue colour formed by reduction of phosphotungstomolybdic acid present in Folin-Denis reagent in alkaline solution. The absorbance of samples was read at 760 nm. Tannic acid was used as the standard and results were expressed as tannic acid equivalent (Schander,1970).

3.8.2 Antioxidant activity of immature, mature and ripe jackfruits

Antioxidants are nutritive or non-nutritive substances present in food. They exert their mode of action by suppressing the formation of reactive oxygen species either by inhibition of enzymes or by chelating trace elements. This technique was employed while assessing the antioxidant activity of jackfruit at different stages of maturity.

3.8.2.1 DPPH Assay

The antioxidant assay was carried out according to the procedure of Yu *et al.*, (2002), DPPH (2,2-diphenyl-1-picryl-hydrazyl) free radical scavenging method was based on electron-transfer that produces a violet solution in methanol. This free radical, stable at room temperature, was reduced in the presence of an antioxidant molecule, giving rise to colourless methanol solution.

3.8.2.2 Phosphomolybdenum Assay

Total antioxidant activity was estimated using phosphomolybdenum assay (Prieto *et al.* 1999). The total antioxidant assay is based on reduction of Phosphate-Molybdenum (VI) to Phosphate-Molybdenum (V) by the sample analyte and the subsequent formation of a green phosphate Molybdenum (V) complex at acidic pH. Extracts were incubated with the Molybdenum (VI) for 90 min at 95°C, the presence of antioxidant components in the extract was assessed by recording the absorbance at 695 nm to detect the reduced green molybdenum complex.

3.9 ANTIDIABETIC PROPERTY OF JACKFRUIT AT DIFFERENT STAGES OF MATURITY

Antidiabetic activity is capacity of lowering blood glucose level through different mechanisms of action.

3.9.1 α-Amylase inhibition activity (Bernfield, 1951)

One hundred μl of buffer (0.02 mol/L sodium phosphate buffer, pH 6.9), 100 μl of α-amylase (EC 3.2.1.1) and 100 μl of starch-water (1 g/100 ml) was added to 100 μl of methanolic extract of jackfruit. Control was prepared in similar way except addition of jackfruit methanolic extract. All the reagents were prepared with phosphate buffer (pH 6.9). After the incubation at 25 °C for 30 min, the reaction was stopped with 1.0 ml of dinitrosalicylic acid reagent. The test tubes were then incubated in boiling water bath for five min and cooled to room temperature. The reaction mixture was then diluted with the addition of 5.4 ml of distilled water and the absorbance was measured at 540 nm. The readings were compared with the control, which contained buffer instead of sample extract. Based on the absorbance value, the per cent inhibition activity was calculated and expressed in percentage.

$$\%\text{inhibition} = [(\text{Abs}_{control}-\text{Abs}_{samples})/ \text{Abs}_{control}] \times 100$$

3.9.2 α-Glucosidase inhibition activity (Apostolidis et al. 2007)

One hundred μl of jackfruit methanolic extract and 100 μl of 0.1 mol/L phosphate buffer (pH 6.9) containing α-glucosidase solution (1 unit/ml) were taken in three tubes for triplicate analysis and pre-incubated at 25 °C for five minute. After the pre-incubation, 100 ml of five mMol/L *p*-nitrophenyl-α-D-glucopyranoside solution prepared in 0.1 mol/L phosphate buffer (pH 6.9) was added to all three tubes and the reaction mixture was incubated at 25 °C for five minute. Similar treatments were given to control except addition of jackfruit methanolic extract. Sample tubes were diluted 10 times with distilled water and the absorbancy was recorded at 405 nm and compared with control. The results were calculated and expressed as percentage of α-glucosidase inhibition.

$$\%inhibition = [(Abs_{control}-Abs_{samples})/ Abs_{control}] \times 100$$

3.9.3 Predicted glycemic index (pGI)

IVSD was estimated as indicated in 3.6.2. The hydrolysis at 90 min was used to predict glycemic index (pGI) using the following formula (Goni *et al.*, 1997).

$$pGI = [39.21 + 0.803(H\ 90)]$$

The jackfruit at different stages of maturity was classified as low GI $\leq$ 55, medium GI = 55-69, and high GI $\geq$ 70 (Allen *et al.*, 2012).

3.10 VALUE ADDITION TO JACKFRUIT OF DIFFERENT STAGES OF MATURITY

3.10.1 Preparation of jackfruit flour

Immature jackfruit was cleaned, peeled, washed and cut into small cubes. Cubes were spread evenly in aluminium mesh tray and dried in food dehydrator at 45-50 °C. Dried cubes were milled in domestic mill. Similarly, mature jackfruit was cleaned and cut into half, the parts like bulb, rags, core and rind were separated. Seeds were removed from the bulbs. In aluminium tray parchment paper was spread and bulbs were arranged evenly. Tray was placed in food dehydrator at 45-50 °C and bulbs dried. Dried bulbs were milled in domestic mill. The preparation of jackfruit flour is depicted in Fig. 3. Flour was stored in air tight containers for further use.

3.10.1.1 Physicochemical properties of jackfruit flour

Physicochemical properties like flour yield, bulk density, pH, total titratable acidity, particle size distribution were estimated for the jackfruit flour

a. Flour yield

Flour obtained after milling was weighed and yield per 100 g of fresh fruits was calculated and expressed in percentage.

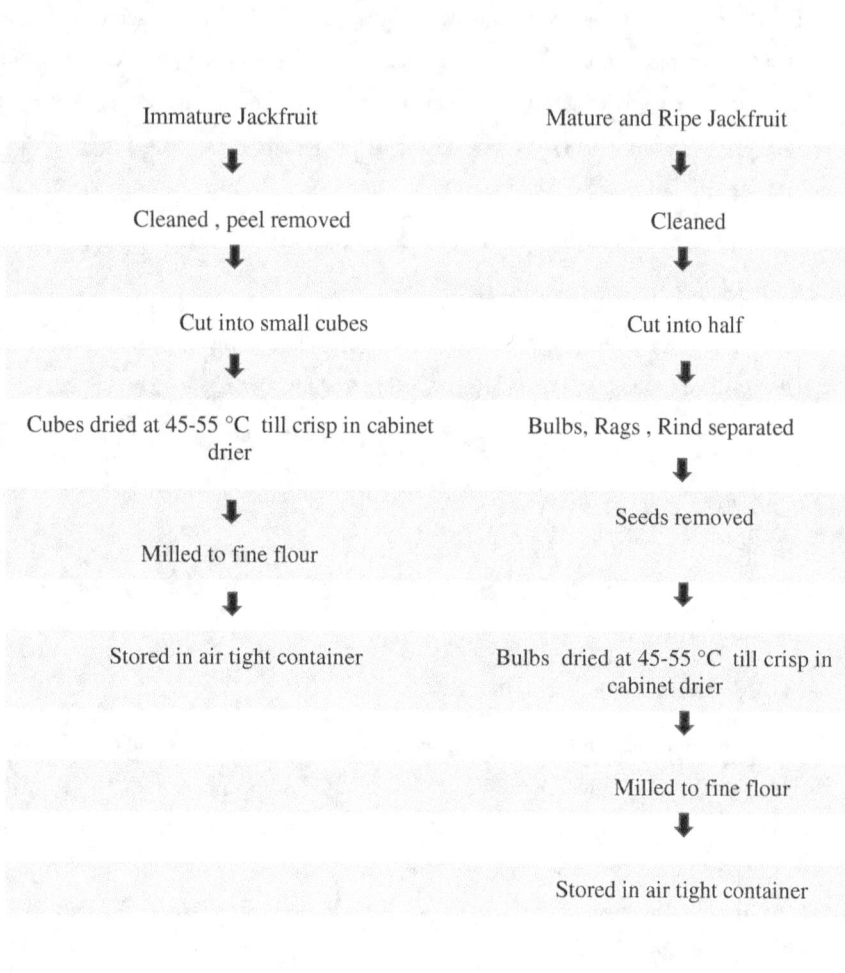

Immature Jackfruit   Mature and Ripe Jackfruit

Cleaned , peel removed   Cleaned

Cut into small cubes   Cut into half

Cubes dried at 45-55 °C till crisp in cabinet drier   Bulbs, Rags , Rind separated

Seeds removed

Milled to fine flour

Stored in air tight container   Bulbs dried at 45-55 °C till crisp in cabinet drier

Milled to fine flour

Stored in air tight container

Fig. 3. Flow chart for the preparation of jackfruit flour

b. Bulk density

Fifty grams of the sample was transferred to 100 ml measuring cylinder. The cylinder was tapped continuously until a constant volume was obtained. The bulk density was calculated as weight of sample (g) for every ml of sample after tapping (Okaka and Potter, 1979).

$$Bulk\ Density\ (g/ml) = \frac{weight\ of\ flour\ (g)}{volume\ of\ flour\ (ml)}$$

c. pH determination

Ten g of sample was mixed in100 ml of CO_2 free distilled water. The mixture was allowed to stand for 15 min, shaken at every five min interval and filtered through Whatman No. 14 filter paper. The pH of the filtrate was measured using a pH meter (Anon, 2000).

d. Total titratable acidity

Ten ml aliquots (triplicates) were pipetted from the filtrate used for pH estimation and titrated against 0.1 M NaOH using phenolphthalein as indicator and the acidity was calculated as per cent lactic acid (Anon, 2000).

e. Particle size distribution

One hundred gram of flour was weighed and passed through sieves of different meshes of BSS standards from 60, 85, 100, 150, 200, 240 and 300 with sieve opening of 250, 180, 150, 105, 75, 63 and 53 microns respectively. The sample was passed from bigger to smaller mesh size. The sample above the sieve was weighed and the readings were recorded.

f. Color of jackfruit flour

Prepared jackfruit flour was analysed for color strength (L* a* b*). Value L* represents lightness/ darkness, value a* represents redness/greeness while value b* indicates yellowness/ blueness of the sample. It was estimated using color spectrophotometer (Konica Minolta Spectrophotometer) with interface JAYPAK 4808.

3.10.1.2 Functional properties of jackfruit flour

Functional properties like water absorption capacity, oil absorption capacity, swelling power and solubility were estimated for jackfruit flour.

a. Water absorption capacity

Water absorption capacity was assessed by the method of Quin and Paton (1983) with modifications. To estimate water absorption capacity, five g of flour was weighed in a 50 ml centrifuge tube and 30 ml of water was added and stirred with a glass rod for five min. After allowing the contents to stand for 30 min, at ambient conditions (temperature 27 °C and relative humidity 65 %), the tubes were centrifuged at 1000 rpm for 25 min. The volume of free liquid was measured and the retained volume was expressed as per cent of water absorbed, on a dry basis.

$$\text{Water absorption capacity, WAC (\%)} = \frac{w2 - w1}{weight\ of\ the\ sample} X\ 100$$

W2–Weight of the wet sample with centrifuge tube

W1- Weight of the dry sample with centrifuge tube

b. Oil absorption capacity

A method given by Sosulski *et al.* (1976) was used to determine oil absorption capacity. Sample (1 g) was mixed with 10 ml of vegetable oil in pre-weighed centrifuge tubes. The tubes were stirred for one min for complete dispersion of sample in the oil. After 30 min of holding time at room temperature (27 °C), the sample was centrifuged at 3000 rpm for 25 min. The separated oil was then removed and tubes were inverted on oil absorbent paper for 25 min to drain the oil. The weight of the tube was recorded. The oil absorption capacity was expressed as grams of oil absorbed per gram of the sample.

$$\text{Oil absorption capacity, OAC (\%)} = \frac{w2 - w1}{weight\ of\ the\ sample} X\ 100$$

W2 –Weight of the wet sample with centrifuge tube

W1- Weight of the dry sample with centrifuge tube

c. Swelling power and solubility

The swelling power and per cent solubility were determined according to the method used by Schoch (1964). Five hundred mg (W_1) of sample was added to a centrifuge tube, weight of centrifuge tube and test sample was noted (W_2). After addition of 20 ml (V_E) distilled water, the centrifuge tube was placed in the water bath at 100°C for 20-30 min till the contents were cooked. Then it was centrifuged at 5000 rpm for 10 min. The supernatant was transferred to a test tube and the inner side of the centrifuge tube was dried well and weighed (W_3). The swelling power of flour was calculated as follows.

$$\text{Swelling power (g/ g)} = \frac{w3 - w2}{w1} X 1$$

For per cent solubility, weight of dried moisture cup was noted (W_4) and after transferring 10 ml aliquot (V_A) in the dish, it was dried at 110°C for 4-5 hr. The moisture dish was cooled and weighed (W_5).

$$\text{Solubility (\%)} = \frac{(W5 - W4)VE}{VA} X \frac{100}{w1}$$

3.10.2 Development of antidiabetic composite mix

Diabetes can be easily managed with modifications in life style and food intake. Foods having low GI and GL are considered suitable for diabetic population. An attempt was rendered to prepare composite mix based on jackfruit flour having antidiabetic properties.

3.10.2.1 Formulation of antidiabetic composite mix

Composite flour was formulated using jackfruit flour, wheat flour and spices. Spices were added to impart flavour to the mix and to act as antidiabetic agent. Jackfruit flour was prepared using the method explained in 3.10.1.Whole wheat flour was purchased from local market. Spices were purchased and processed as needed. All the ingredients were mixed in different proportions (10:90 20:80, 30:70, 40:60, 50:50, 60:40 and 70:30 of jackfruit flour and wheat flour and keeping the spices constant). The composite antidiabetic mix was converted to *chapathi* and served to ten trained panel members for sensory evaluation. Nine point hedonic scale (Peryam and Girardot, 1952) was used for scoring the appearance, color, flavour, taste, texture, overall acceptability. The acceptability index was calculated based on total score. Best formulation of composite mix in terms of acceptability was further used to study the functional properties, antidiabetic assay, proximate principles, nutritional quality, nutritional efficacy, glycemic index and storage.

3.10.2.2 Colour and particle size of developed antidiabetic composite mix

Jackfruit based antidiabetic composite mix was analysed for color strength (L* a* b*). Value L* represents lightness/ darkness, value a* represents redness/ greenness while value b* indicates yellowness/ blueness of the sample. It is done using color spectrophotometer (Konica Minolta Spectrophotometer) with interface JAYPAK 4808.

To assess distribution of particle size, one hundred gram of the developed mix was weighed and passed through sieves of different meshes of BSS standards from 60, 85, 100, 150, 200, 240 and 300 with sieve opening of 250, 180, 150, 105, 75, 63 and 53 microns respectively. The sample was passed from bigger to smaller mesh size. The sample above the sieve was weighed and the readings were recorded.

3.10.2.3 Functional properties of antidiabetic composite mix

Water absorption capacity, oil absorption capacity, swelling power and solubility of the composite mix were analysed as detailed in 3.10.1.2.

3.10.2.4 Proximate composition of developed composite mix

Composite mix was analysed for moisture, protein, fat, ash, crude fibre the amounts of carbohydrate and energy present in the mix were calculated as detailed in 3.5.2.

3.10.2.5 Nutritional quality of developed composite mix

In-vitro protein digestibility of composite flour was estimated as detailed in 3.7.1.*In-vitro* starch digestibility of composite flour and starch digestibility index (SDI) were assessed as per detailed procedure given in 3.7.2.

3.10.2.6 Antioxidant components and activity of developed composite mix

Dietary fiber content was estimated as outlined in 3.6.5. The antioxidant components and activity were estimated as outlined in 3.8.1 and 3.8.2.

3.11 STORAGE QUALITY OF DEVELOPED COMPOSITE MIX

Shelf life study of developed composite flour was conducted in order to maximize the usage of flour and make the flour available for longer period of time. Effect of storage on moisture content, antioxidant activity, sensory quality and microbial activity were analyzed. Composite flour (250 g) was packed individually in two packaging material *i.e* 160 gauge polyethylene (HDPE) and foil coated pouches (ALPE) and stored at ambient temperature (25 -30°) for period of 180 days.

3.11.1 Effect of storage on moisture content of developed composite mix

Samples were drawn at 15 days interval and assessed for moisture content in triplicates by AOAC method (Anon, 2000). Results were recorded, moisture content of flour and increase in moisture compared to zero day of storage was calculated and expressed in percentage.The procedure followed is given in **3.5.2.1**

3.11.2 Effect of storage on sensory parameters of developed composite mix

The samples were drawn at interval of every 15 days. The flour was converted to chapathi and subjected to sensory evaluation by a trained panel of judges (10 no.) of the department of Food Science and Nutrition. Using nine point hedonic scale the appearance, texture, color, flavour, taste and over all acceptability were scored (Peryam t tt r tone ,1955).

3.11.3 Effect of storage on antioxidant activity of developed composite mix

The samples were drawn at every 30 days interval and tested for antioxidant activity by DPPH Assay and Phosphomolybdenum Assay as explained in 3.8.2. Results were recorded, antioxidant activity of flour and change in antioxidant activity compared to zero day of storage was calculated and expressed in percentage.

3.11.4 Effect of storage on microbial quality of developed composite mix

Microbial analysis for counts of bacteria, fungi, *E-coli* and actinomycetes was carried out monthly by total plate count method. The media used were nutrient agar, Rose Bengal Agar and Eosin Methylene Blue (EMB) agar, respectively. The technique used was pour plate method as described by Diliello (1982). The sample was serially diluted and the appropriate aliquots were poured into different plates, then respective molten cool medium was poured separately and mixed uniformly by swirling the plates. This ensures uniform distribution of microbial cells as the medium gradually cools and solidifies in plate. On solidification of medium the plates were inverted and incubated at 37 ± 1 °C. The observations were recorded after 24 hr of incubation for bacteria and E-coli and after four to five days for fungi. Average counts of replications were expressed as number of Colony Forming Units (CFU)/g of sample by using following formula.

$$CFU/g = \frac{Number\ of\ colonies\ * dilution\ factor}{Weight\ of\ sample}$$

3.12 EFFICACY OF THE DEVELOPED DIABETIC MIX IN CONTROLLING BLOOD GLUCOSE

The efficacy of developed mix in controlling rise in blood glucose level was tested in terms of Glycemic Index. The glycemic index was assessed both *in-vitro* and *in-vivo* methods.

3.12.1 Antidiabetic assay of developed composite mix

Antidiabetic assay of developed mix was carried out by *in-vitro* methods. Alpha-Amylase inhibition assay was carried out as detailed in 3.9.1. Alpha -glucosidase inhibition assay was estimated as detailed in 3.9.2.

3.12.2 Estimation of *glycemic* index by *in vitro* method:

The glycemic index of the composite mix was predicted using the equation described by Goni *et al.* (1997) employing the IVSD at 90 min.

$$PGI = 39.21 + 0.803 (HI_{90})$$

3.12.3 Estimation of *glycemic* index by *in vivo* method

The glycemic index indicates the extent of rise in blood sugar in response to a test food in comparison with an equivalent dose of glucose. The study was conducted on non-diabetic healthy volunteers. Age, gender and anthropometric measurements of the selected volunteers were noted. Fasting blood glucose test was performed on all the healthy volunteers who were between 25 to 35 years of their age and examined in the morning after 12 hour fast. After the initial drawing of blood sample participants were asked to drink a calibrated dose (50 g of glucose) within 5 min with 200ml of water and asked to sit quietly throughout the test. Blood samples were drawn at every 30 min up to 120 min (plus or minus 2-3 minutes) after drinking the glucose. Volunteers were instructed not to consume heavy meal a day before the test and to maintain gap of 12 h from last meal to GTT. All were requested to come empty stomach in the morning. After one week of wash out period, Meal Tolerance Test (MTT) was designed to be performed in the morning (between 9 and 10 A.M.) after an overnight fast, with no food or drink (with the exception of water) and no smoking after 10 P.M. the preceding day. Volunteers consumed a 50g carbohydrate test food "*chapathi*" with mango pickle within 10 min. Blood samples for glucose were taken before eating and then at intervals of every 30 min up to 120 min (plus or minus 2-3 minutes). Each time the capillary blood glucose level was estimated using Glucometer (BG-03). The blood glucose response curves were plotted for both oral Glucose Tolerance Test (GTT) and the test carbohydrate meal (MTT). The glycemic index was calculated using the formula given by Wolver and Jenkins (1986).

$$\text{Glycemic Index (GI)} = \frac{Area\ under\ glucose\ curve\ of\ test\ meal}{Area\ under\ glucose\ curve\ of\ reference} \times 100$$

Classification of glycemic index (Brand-Miller, 2002)

< 55 – low

56 -69 – medium

>70 - high

Glycemic load (GL) was calculated using the formula GI x available carbohydrate per serving divided by 100 (Venn and green 2007). GL was categorized as low (≤10), medium (less than 10–20) or high (more than 20).

3.13 ACCEPTABILITY OF DEVELOPED PRODUCT AMONG DIABETIC SUBJECTS

3.13.1 Selection of diabetic subjects

Minimum 30 subjects who were diabetic for at least ten years were selected for the study. Basic information regarding name, age, address etc. And specific information like history of diabetes, medicines consumed, life style modification, foods consumed etc., was collected using questionnaire developed for the purpose.

3.13.2 Preparation of product

Chapathi was prepared from composite mix and one serving (50g of raw flour) was served to the selected subjects with pickle during brunch time (between 10.00 to 11.30 am).

3.13.3 Collection of feedback about diabetic food

FACT Scale (Schutz, 1964) was used to know the acceptability and interest in the designed food. The opinion of the diabetic population selected for the acceptability was collected. The perception of the subjects regarding satiety, any kind of discomfort and general opinion were collected.

3.14 COST ANALYSIS OF VALUE ADDED JACKFRUIT BASED PRODUCTS

The cost analysis of mature jackfruit flour and antidiabetic composite mix includes the purchase and economic feasibility of production and sales. The cost for production of 5 kg and 50kg was calculated considering the materials and cost involved in processing, packaging and depreciation value of fixed cost material

3.15 STATISTICAL ANALYSIS

The documented data of respondents of jackfruit was expressed in number and percentage. The observation recorded for physical and chemical characteristics of jackfruit at three stages of maturity were analysed by one way ANOVA. The nutritional, antioxidant components, antioxidant activity of jackfruit at three stages of maturity were analysed by one way ANOVA. Student 's 't' test was used to know the significant difference between jackfruit flour and composite mix. Two way ANOVA was used to know the changes in product during storage. Duncan's new multiple range test (DMRT) was used to determine significant differences. Correlations among the data was obtained using Pearson's correlation coefficient. These statistical analysis were carried out using IBM SPSS software version 18.0 and MS Excel 2013. Wherever significant results obtained the critical difference test was used (Steel and Torrie, 1960).

CHAPTER -4

EXPERIMENTAL RESULTS

India is second largest country in the world producing highest amounts and types of fruits and vegetables owing to huge diversity in flora and fauna. Because of regional differences there are many fruits and vegetables which are underutilized in-spite of being nutritious and having rich therapeutic value. Jackfruit is one among them, well known fruit utilized only in the areas of production. Immature fruit is consumed as vegetable whereas the mature and ripe stage is widely used for table purpose or for processing into different products. The fruit immature, mature or ripe stage contains good amount of fibre, carotenoids and many other nutraceutical components. Hence to understand and explore the therapeutic value of jackfruit, present study was undertaken to study the composition, health benefits and value addition to the fruit of different stages of maturity.

4.1 INFORMATION ABOUT JACKFRUIT

Jackfruit is well known in Western Ghats but its utilization is limited; it can be consumed in all stages of maturity. The information related to consumption, utilization and storage, locally prepared recipes; traditional knowledge of therapeutic significance, types of processing of jackfruit has been collected and presented in tables 1 to 4.

The general information of the subjects selected for collecting information on jackfruits is presented in Table 1. The 25 subjects included 19 males and six females, with age ranging from 30 to 65 years. Major source of income was farming for all the members. Jackfruit was utilized in many ways. All selected subjects (100%) used the fruit for self consumption, while, 64 per cent of them sold at different stages of maturity. Sixty eight per cent of the subjects preserved for future use while, 28 per cent of them were involved in commercialization of fruit and fruit products. During season (November to June), jackfruit was consumed daily. The jackfruit of different stages was consumed in different forms *viz,*. cooked, roasted seeds, ripe fruit, unprocessed, processed, preserved and fermentation.

4.1.1 Therapeutic properties, local preparations and methods of processing

It can be seen from Table 2 that jackfruit was consumed in four different ailments or conditions *viz*. constipation, cold and cough, baby food and eye sight. Young and mature jackfruit was consumed in boiled form for relief from constipation, while roasted seeds were

Table 1 General information about jackfruit

Total no. of families	25
Age group	30 -65
Gender Male Female	 19 06
Major Source of income	Farming
Utilization of jackfruit	1. Self-consumption (100%) 2. Sale at different stages of maturity (64%) 3. Preserve for future and do commercialization of fruit (68%) 4. Commercialization of fruit and fruit product (28%)
Frequency of consuming jackfruit	1. During season (November to June) almost every day 2. Other than season weekly once or twice
Form of Consumption	Cooked, roasted seeds, ripe fruit, unprocessed, Processed, Preserved, Fermented

Table 2 Perceived therapeutic properties of jackfruit

Aliments (n=25)	Stage of consumption	Form of consumption
Constipation (26%)*	Young and mature jackfruit	Boiled
Cold and cough (33%)*	Seeds	Roasted
Baby food (39%)*	Seed (Powder)	Roasted
Eye sight (22%)*	Ripe fruit	Unprocessed

*Multiple answers were received

consumed during cold and cough. Roasted seeds in powder form were given as supplementary foods to babies whereas, ripe fruit was perceived to improve eye sight.

Table 3 shows types of local preparations of jackfruit at different stages of maturity. Various foods prepared included *sambhar* (100%), *dosa* (56%), *idli* (32%), *paddu/ kadbu* (32%), jackfruit *bhath* (48%), pickle (40%), papad (80%), chips (100%) and *laddu/modak* (20%). *Sambhar* and pickle were prepared with young and mature jackfruit. *Dosa, idli* and *paddu* were prepared with unripe and ripe jackfruit. Jackfruit *bhath* was prepared with young jackfruit. Papad and chips were prepared in mature stage, while, *laddu/ modak* were prepared with ripe fruits. Pickle, chips, papad and *laddu/modak* were prepared for self consumption and for sale, while other products were for domestic consumption.

Table 4 records methods of preservation of jackfruit practiced generally. Young jackfruit was preserved in the form of pickle (sweet/salty). Fresh bulbs of mature jackfruit were preserved in carboys with salt. Jackfruit was preserved as jam or leather in ripe stage. Raw jackfruit seeds were preserved in sun dried form and also as roasted form in air tight container.

4.2 PHYSICO-CHEMICAL CHARACTERISTICS OF JACKFRUITS OF DIFFERENT STAGES OF MATURITY

Physical properties of fruits or any food are the properties which gives perceptible characteristics and basic component. Ten fruits were used to know the basic characteristics for understanding its nature and functionality.

4.2.1 Physical properties of jackfruit at different stages of maturity

The physical properties of different stages of jackfruit viz. immature, mature and ripe are presented in Table 5. The average length of immature, mature and ripe jackfruit was 11.7 cm, 47.18 cm and 44.2 cm respectively whereas; average breadth for the afore mentioned stages was 13.35 cm, 26.12 cm and 25.51 cm. The average length-wise circumference of the three stages was 53.63 cm, 94.04 cm and 94.08 cm respectively whereas the width-wise circumference was 80.95 cm, 70.04 cm and 74.47 cm. Approximately, 30.75 percent of the jackfruit was inedible in the immature stage and remaining 69.25 percent was edible. Similarly, the percentage of edible and inedible portions of mature and ripe jackfruit was 56.96 and 32.76, 28.51 and 59.28 respectively. The seeds were not mature enough to be

Table 3 Types of local preparations of jackfruit at different stages of maturity

List of foods	No of respondents	Stage of jackfruit used for products	Purpose of preparation
Sambhar	25 (100)	Young and mature jackfruit	Domestic consumption
Dosa	14 (56)	Unripe and ripe jackfruit	Domestic consumption
Idli	08 (32)	Unripe and ripe jackfruit	Domestic consumption
Paddu /*Kadbu*	08 (32)	Unripe and ripe jackfruit	Domestic consumption
Jackfruit Bhath	12 (48)	Young Jackfruit	Domestic consumption
Pickle	10 (40)	Young and mature jackfruit	Domestic consumption and sale
Papad	20 (80)	Mature jackfruit	Domestic consumption and sale
Chips	25 (100)	Mature jackfruit	Domestic consumption and sale
Laddu /modak	05 (20)	Ripe jackfruit	Domestic consumption and sale

Note: multiple responses given by respondents; figures in parenthesis indicate percentages

Table 4 Methods of preservation of jackfruit practiced by respondents

Stage of jackfruit	Method of Preservation
Young jackfruit	Pickle (sweet/ salty)
Mature jackfruit	Fresh bulbs of jackfruit preserved in carboys with good amount of salt
Ripe	Jam or leather
Seeds	Sun dried raw/ roasted in air tight container

Table 5 Physical properties of jackfruit at different stages of maturity

Properties	Stages of maturity of jackfruit			F Value	S.Em	CD
	Immature	Mature	Ripe			
Length (cm)	11.7 ±1.13^b	47.18 ± 5.15^a	44.20 ± 4.36^a	247.672	1.250	3.629*
Breadth (cm)	13.35 ±1.31^b	26.12 ± 1.46^a	25.51 ±1.44^a	261.201	0.445	1.293*
Length wise circumference (cm)	53.63 ±1.21^b	94.04 ± 6.84^a	94.08 ± 0.96^a	743.737	1.315	3.818*
Width wise circumference (cm)	80.95 ±0.83^a	70.04 ±1.49^c	74.47 ±0.70^b	3136.018	0.526	1.527*
Weight of seed (kg)	NF	0.84 ±0.06 (10.26)	0.92 ± 0.00 (12.20)	1613.482	0.014	NS
Weight of edible portion (kg)	2.05 ±0.6^b (69.25)	4.66 ±0.32^a (56.96)	2.15 ± 0.34^b (28.51)	63.096	0.177	0.515*
Weight of inedible portion	0.91 ± 0.05^c (30.75)	2.68 ±0.56^b (32.76)	4.47 ± 0.45^a (59.28)	8.199	0.402	1.169*

Note: values are average of ten fruits; NF: seeds not mature enough to be separated
Figures in parenthesis indicate percentages;SEm- Standard Error Mean,
CD- Critical Difference, NS- Non Significant, * Significant @5%,
Values with the same superscripts (a, b) in the same row are not significantly different (p≤0.01).

separated in the immature stage. The average weight of seeds in mature and ripe stages was 0.84 kg and 0.92 kg respectively. ANOVA test indicated that length, breadth and length-wise circumference were significantly lower in immature fruit, while, mature and ripe fruits were on par with each other. Seed weight of mature and ripe fruit did not differ significantly (Plate 3).

4.2.2 Proximate composition of jackfruit at different stages of maturity

A perusal of Table 6 indicates that moisture in jackfruit in the three stages viz. immature, mature and ripe was 70.61, 68.43 and 76.20 respectively with ripe fruit having significantly higher value (76.20%) and mature having significantly lower (68.43%). Protein content was found to be maximum (4.36%) in mature followed by immature (3.42%). Minimum protein content was found in ripe fruit (1.61%). Crude fat values (%) for the three stages were 4.16, 2.43 and 1.76 respectively, being significantly maximum in immature and minimum in ripe. The ash and crude fiber contents of immature and ripe fruit were statistically on par with each other (3.15 & 2.99 and 9.96 & 10.10% respectively). However, crude fiber was lower in mature fruits and ash was higher than other two stages. The total and available carbohydrates were significantly higher in ripe (93.64 & 83.54% respectively) followed by mature (89.68 & 82.52% respectively) and immature (89.27 & 79.31% respectively) fruits. The energy content (kcal) in the three stages were found to be 368, 369 and 357 respectively, mature having maximum and ripe having minimum.

4.2.3 The mineral content of jackfruit at different stages of maturity

The mineral content of jackfruit at different stages of maturity is given in Table 7. All the minerals estimated were higher in immature jackfruit followed by mature, while ripe fruits were having lowest mineral contents. The calcium content ranged from 36.75 to 55.30 mg/100g; iron ranged from 0.34 to 2.75 mg/100g; zinc from 0.09 to 2.44; copper from 0.20 to 2.00mg/100g. Manganese content of both mature and ripe jackfruit was 0.36mg/100g, whereas immature fruit contained 0.94mg/100g. The mineral contents of all three stages were statistically different.

4.3 CARBOHYDRATE PROFILE OF JACKFRUIT AT DIFFERENT STAGES OF MATURITY

Carbohydrates are important nutrient present in any food; presence of carbohydrate gives structure, taste, aroma and plays an essential role in food preparation and processing.

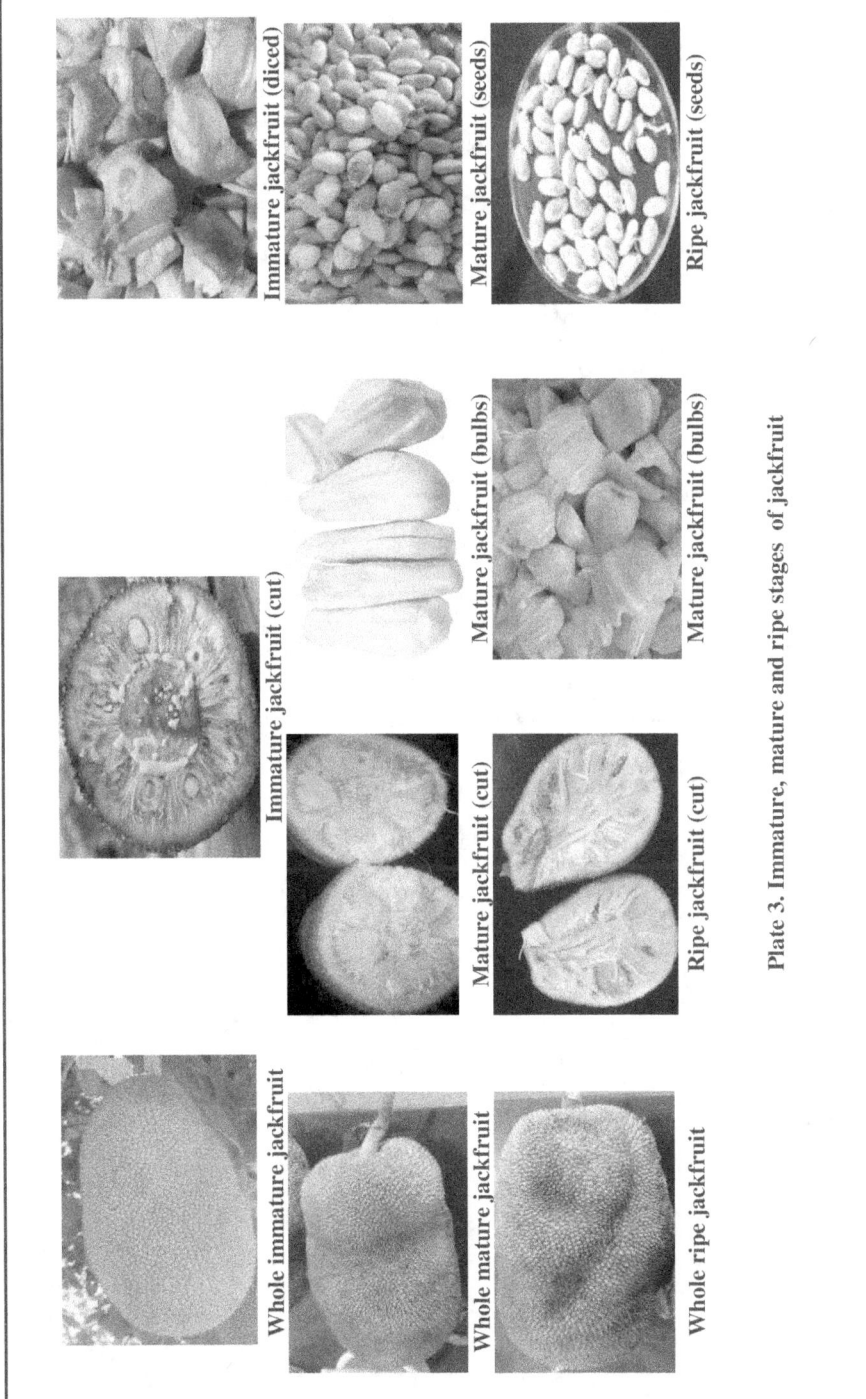

Plate 3. Immature, mature and ripe stages of jackfruit

Table 6 Proximate principles (dwb) of jackfruit at different stages of maturity

Proximate principles (%)	Stages of maturity of jackfruit			F Value	S.Em	CD
	Immature	Mature	Ripe			
Moisture	70.61±0.0^b	68.43±0.08^c	76.20±42.2^a	313.07	0.228	0.789*
Protein	3.42±0.08^b	4.36±0.06^a	1.61±0.02^c	2126.07	0.025	0.089*
Crude Fat	4.16±0.05^a	2.43±0.04^b	1.76±0.05^c	11.645	0.065	0.227*
Ash	3.15±0.02^b	3.53±0.01^a	2.99±0.16^b	1665.52	0.036	0.126*
Crude fiber	9.96±0.01^a	7.16±0.13^b	10.10±0.2^a	76.382	0.179	0.622*
Total Carbohydrate	89.27 ±0.02	89.68±0.02	93.64±0.03	52011.04	0.012	0.372*
Available Carbohydrate	79.31±0.15	82.52±0.25	83.54±0.05	44301.79	0.057	2.58*
Energy (Kcal)	368±0.04	369±0.05	357±0.13	1574.519	0.018	2.58*

Note: Values are the mean of three replications, S.Em- Standard Error Mean,
CD- Critical Difference, NS- Non Significant, * Significant @5%,
Values with the same superscripts (a, b) in the same row are not significantly different (p≤0.01)

Table 7 Mineral content (dwb) of jackfruit at different stages of maturity

Minerals (mg/ 100g)	Stages of maturity of jackfruit			F Value	SEm	CD
	Immature	Mature	Ripe			
Calcium	55.30±0.28^a	44.67±0.50^b	36.75±0.03^c	2369.84	0.19	0.66***
Iron	2.75±0.04^a	0.39±0.025^b	0.34±0.01^b	7342.07	0.02	0.06***
Zinc	2.44±0.01^a	0.19±0.019^b	0.09±0.02^c	18458.19	0.01	0.02***
Copper	2.00±0.25^a	0.24±0.02^b	0.20±0.05^b	145.39	0.09	0.30***
Manganese	0.94±0.08^a	0.36±0.03^b	0.36±.015^b	133.30	0.03	0.11***

Note: Values are the mean of three replications, SEm- Standard Error Mean,
CD- Critical Difference, NS- Non Significant, *Significant @0.1%
Values with the same superscripts (a, b) in the same row are not significantly different (p≤0.01)

Carbohydrate can be in the form of isolated molecule or in physical association with other molecules. Carbohydrate can be present in foods in many forms like sugars, starch, cellulose etc. Amount and type of carbohydrate presents in food decides the glycemic index and glycemic load of any food substance.

4.3.1 Carbohydrate profile of jackfruit at different stages of maturity

Table 8 records the carbohydrate fractions of jackfruit at all three stages of maturity viz. immature, mature and ripe. Total sugar was found to be lowest in immature (0.40%) and highest in ripe (13.03%) fruit. Mature jackfruit was having (2.53%) of total sugars. Analysis of variance indicated significant difference in the total sugar of all the three stages. Immature (0.38%) and mature (0.43%) jackfruit were on par with each other regarding reducing sugar content. On the contrary, ripe jackfruit had significantly higher (8.77%) reducing sugar content. Non reducing sugar was highest in ripe 4.05 per cent while immature (1.04%) and mature (2.00 %) were on par with each other.

Total starch was recorded significantly highest in mature jackfruit (40.50%) followed by immature (30.30%) and ripe (20.70%). Immature and mature stages of jackfruit contained statistically similar amounts of amylose (8.00%) and (7.99%) respectively. While ripe fruit had only traces of amylose (0.02%). Amylopectin was highest in mature (32.54%) followed by immature (22.33%) and ripe (20.70%). The three stages of jackfruit possessed significantly varying amount of amylopectin.

Perusal of table 8 indicates that mature and ripe jackfruit contained statistically similar amounts of resistance starch (16.09%) and (13.13%) respectively. On the contrary immature stage of jackfruit possessed 8.24 per cent of resistant starch which was significantly lower than other two stages.

4.3.2 Dietary fibre of jackfruit at different stages of maturity

Dietary fibre is believed to be best trafficker of antioxidants in human body. Fig 4 shows that total, soluble and insoluble dietary fibre was highest in mature jackfruit (14.7, 9.70 and 5.00% respectively) followed by ripe (9.29, 7.80 &1.48% respectively). Immature jackfruit contained significantly lower value of total (3.60%), soluble (0.93%) and insoluble (2.70%) dietary fiber.

Table 8 Carbohydrate profile (dwb) of jackfruit at different stages of maturity

Carbohydrate fractions (%)	Stages of maturity of jackfruit			F Value	SEm	CD
	Immature	**Mature**	**Ripe**			
Total Sugar	0.40 ± 0.08^c	2.53 ± 0.08^b	13.03 ± 0.06^a	25088.76	0.04	0.14*
Reducing Sugar	0.38 ± 0.09^b	0.43 ± 0.02^b	8.77 ± 0.02^a	22975.45	0.03	0.11*
Non-Reducing Sugar	1.04 ± 0.05^b	2.00 ± 0.03^b	4.05 ± 0.04^a	4255.26	0.09	0.30*
Total Starch	30.30 ± 0.40^b	40.50 ± 0.33^a	20.70 ± 0.04^c	3261.96	0.17	0.60*
Amylose	8.00 ± 2.00^a	7.99 ± 0.08^a	0.02 ± 0.01^b	47.58	0.67	2.31*
Amylopectin	22.33 ± 0.06^b	32.54 ± 0.19^a	20.70 ± 0.07^c	8310.09	0.07	0.24*
Resistant starch	8.24 ± 0.45^b	16.09 ± 2.02^a	13.13 ± 2.07^a	16.49	0.98	3.38*

Note: Values are the mean of three replications, SEm- Standard Error Mean,
CD- Critical Difference, NS- Non Significant, * Significant @5%,
Values with the same superscripts (a, b) in the same row are not significantly different (p≤0.01).

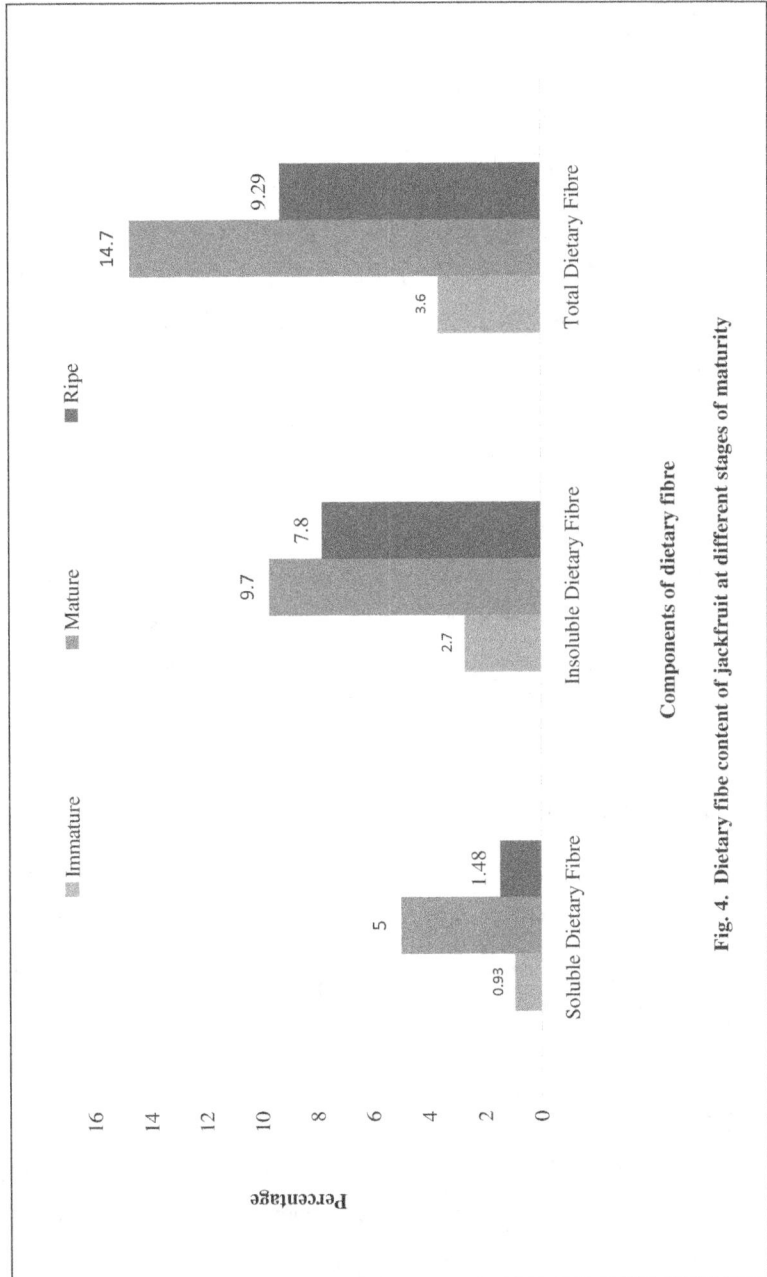

Fig. 4. Dietary fibe content of jackfruit at different stages of maturity

4.4 NUTRITIONAL QUALITY OF JACKFRUIT AT DIFFERENT STAGES OF MATURITY

The results of nutritional quality assessed in terms of protein and starch digestibilities are presented in Fig 5, 6 and Table 9.

4.4.1 *In vitro* protein digestibility of jackfruit at different stages of maturity

Fig 5 depicts the *in vitro* protein digestibility of jackfruit at different stages of maturity. Digestibility of mature jackfruit was highest (91%) followed by ripe (89%) and immature (68%), respectively. Digestibility of all the stages of jackfruit was significantly different from each other.

4.4.2 In vitro starch digestibility of jackfruit at different stages of maturity

In-vitro starch digestibility (%) of jackfruit at different stages of maturity *viz.* immature, mature and ripe at time intervals of 30, 90 and 120 minutes has been recorded in Table 9. The *IVSD* of immature jackfruit was 9.49, 10.52 and 10.54 per cent respectively after 30, 90 and 120 min. of digestion. Respective values for mature stage were 12.53, 19.35 and 12.77 respectively. Ripe fruits of jack exhibited respective values of 11.31, 28.58 and 40.51 per cent. Among the three stages of maturity, ripe jackfruit had significantly higher digestibility at 30 min (11.31%) 90 min (28.58%) and 120 min (40.51%).

4.4.3 Starch digestibility index of jackfruit at different stages of maturity

Starch digestibility index of jackfruit at different level of maturity is expressed in Fig 6. Significantly highest digestibility index was recorded in ripe jackfruit (49.17%) followed by immature fruit (28.19%) and mature fruit (27.84%). However, the index of immature and mature fruits did not differ considerably.

4.5 ANTIOXIDANT COMPONENTS AND ACTIVITY OF JACKFRUIT AT DIFFERENT STAGES OF MATURITY

Antioxidants are the substances that prevent the damage due to oxygen caused by free radicals. The results of antioxidant components and antioxidant capacity analysed by DPPH and phosphomolybdenum assay methods is presented in this section.

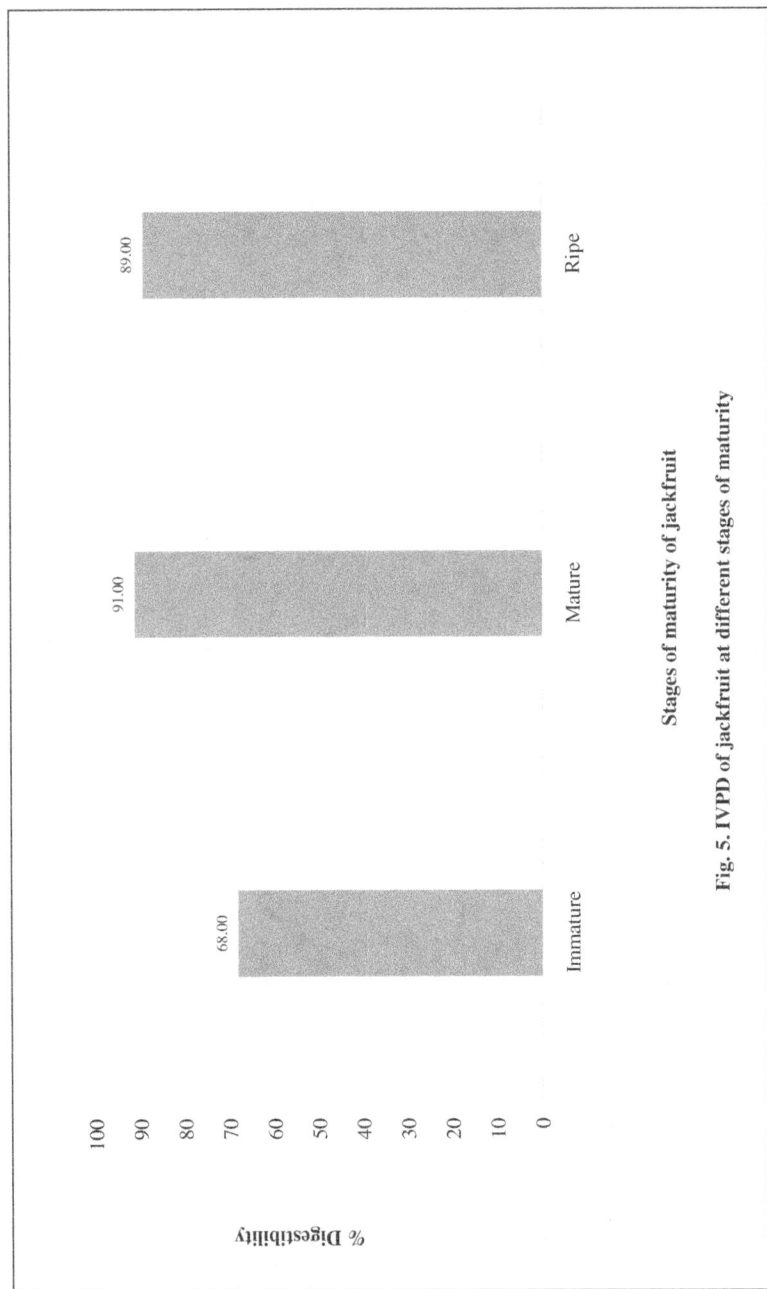

Fig. 5. IVPD of jackfruit at different stages of maturity

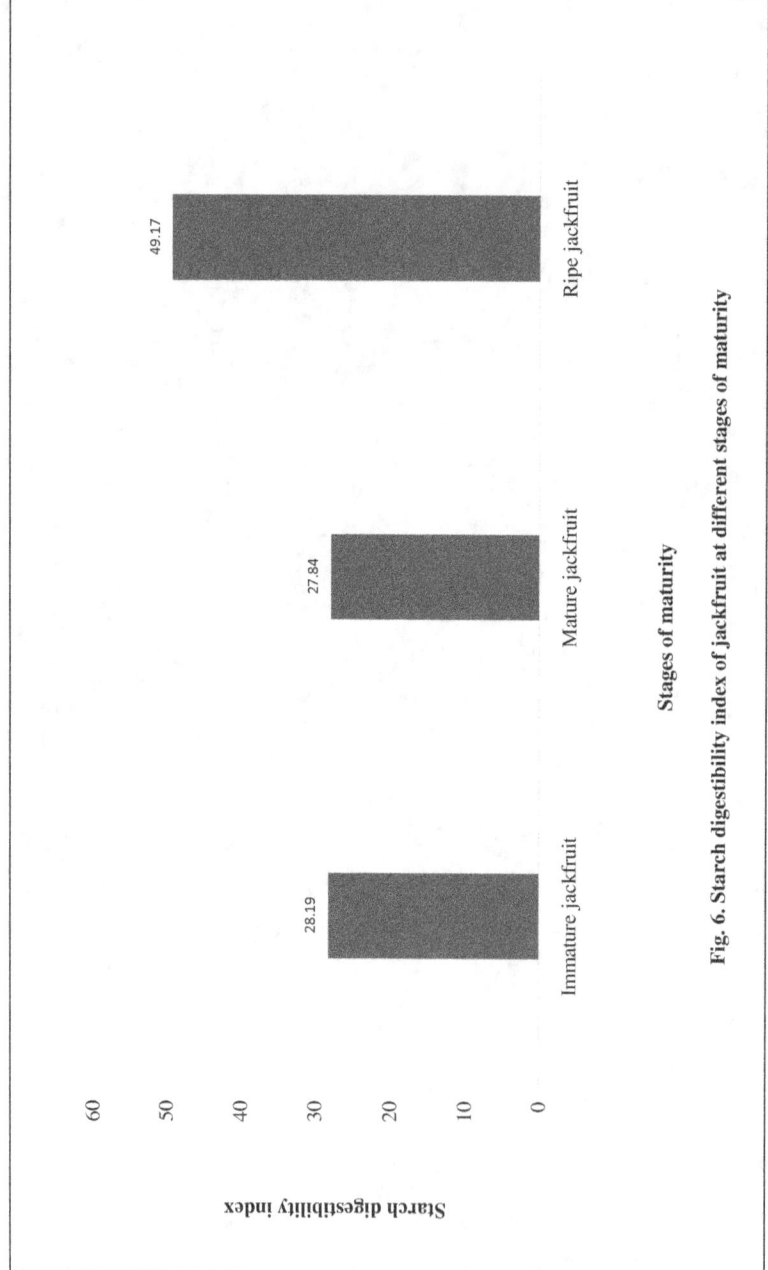

Fig. 6. Starch digestibility index of jackfruit at different stages of maturity

Table 9 *In-vitro* starch digestibility of jackfruit at different stages of maturity

Stages of maturity	*In-vitro* starch digestibility (%)		
	30 min	**90 min**	**120 min**
Immature jackfruit	9.49±0.08[b]	10.52±0.02[c]	10.54±0.92[c]
Mature jackfruit	12.53±0.48[a]	19.35±0.01[b]	12.77±0.98[b]
Ripe jackfruit	11.31±0.87[a]	28.58±0.10[a]	40.51±0.92[a]
F value	21.08	69666.92	951.94
SEm	0.33	0.04	0.54
CD	1.15*	0.13*	1.87*

Note: Values are the mean of three replications, SEm- Standard Error Mean,
CD- Critical Difference, NS- Non Significant, * Significant @5%,
Values with the same superscripts (a, b) in the same column are not significantly different ($p \leq 0.01$).

4.5.1 Antioxidant components of jackfruit at different stages of maturity

Antioxidants are compounds which inhibit the oxidation and removes free radicals by neutralizing them in human body by giving or taking extra electron. Antioxidants also restrict the development of free radical and hoist immunity in the body. Vitamins and mineral rich foods are believed to be rich source of antioxidants.

4.5.1.1 Total phenols and tannins of jackfruit at different stages of maturity

Total phenols and tannin content of jackfruit at different stages of maturity is depicted in Fig 7. Immature jackfruit showed higher amount of total phenols (55.03mgGAE/g) followed by ripe (54.38 mgGAE/g). Tannins was observed to be higher in ripe jackfruit (0.53 mgTAE/g) followed by mature (0.51mgTAE/g). Mature jackfruit contained lower total phenols (49.89 mgGAE/g) while, immature fruit contained lower tannins (0.11mgTAE/g).

4.5.2 Antioxidant activity and capacity of jackfruit at different stages of maturity

Table 10 shows the DPPH (%) and phosphomolybdenum (%) in the jackfruit at three stages of maturity of jackfruit *viz.,* immature, mature and ripe to quantify antioxidants and evaluate antioxidant activity. The values of DPPH and phosphomolybdenum at immature stage were 98.15 per cent and 70.62 per cent respectively. The respective values at mature stage were 67.41 and 61.44 per cent, while the values at ripe stage were 87.14 and 11.34 per cent respectively. It was observed that both DPPH and phosphomolybdenum were significantly higher in immature stage.

4.6 ANTIDIABETIC PROPERTY OF JACKFRUIT AT DIFFERENT STAGES OF MATURITY

The antidiabetic property of jackfruit in terms of inhibition of alpha amylase and alpha glucosidase at different stages of maturity is shown in Fig 8. Inhibition of alpha glucosidase was recorded to be highest in immature jackfruit (95.60%) followed by mature (77.74%) and ripe jackfruit (59.55%). Similar trend was observed in alpha amylase inhibition wherein, immature jackfruit recorded maximum inhibition of 84.60 per cent followed mature (64.72%) and ripe jackfruit (58.76%).

4.6.1 Predicted glycemic index of the jackfruit at different stages of maturity

Glycemic index is a tool which measures the capability of carbohydrates present in foods to rise the blood sugar level in human beings. Glycemic load is an equation that takes

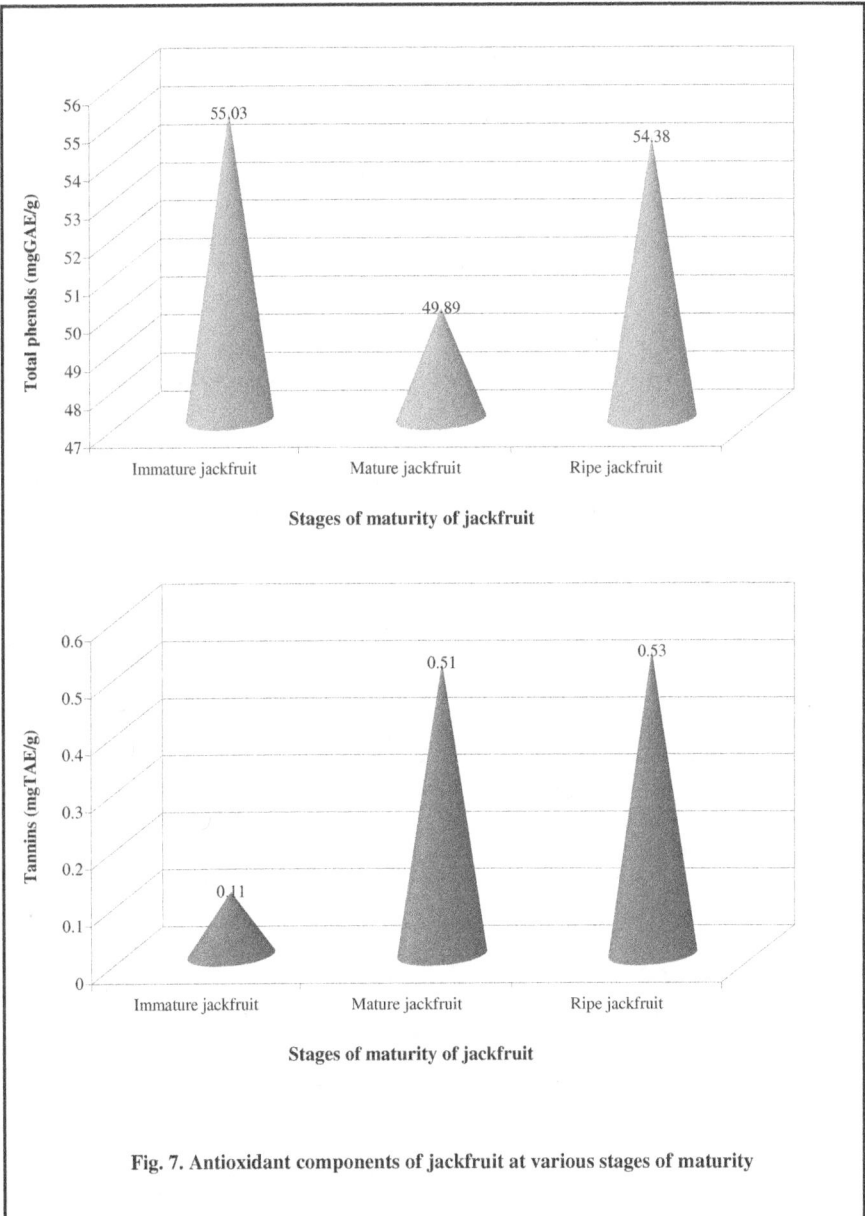

Fig. 7. Antioxidant components of jackfruit at various stages of maturity

Table 10 Antioxidant scavenging activity and total antioxidant activity of jackfruit at different stages of maturity

Stages of maturity	DPPH (%)	Phosphomolybdenum (%)
Immature	98.15 ± 0.03^a	70.62 ± 0.07^a
Mature	67.41 ± 0.06^c	61.44 ± 0.12^b
Ripe	87.14 ± 0.03^b	11.34 ± 0.03^c
F Value	357895.2	453594.2
SEm	0.06	0.11
CD	0.33*	0.16*

Note: Values are the mean of three replications, SEm- Standard Error Mean,
CD- Critical Difference, NS- Non Significant, * Significant @5%,
Values with the same superscripts (a, b) in the same column are not significantly different ($p\leq0.01$).

into account the amount of available carbohydrates present in food as well as the glycemic index of that food.

Predicted glycemic index and glycemic load of jackfruit at different stages of maturity is shown in Fig 9. Lowest glycemic index was recorded in immature stage of jackfruit (47.66%) followed by mature (54.75%) and ripe jackfruit (62.16%).

Total sugar was positively and significantly correlated to reducing, non-reducing sugars and glycemic index (Table 11) while it was negatively and significantly correlated to total starch and amylose. Reducing sugar had significant positive correlation with non-reducing sugars and amylose and had significant negative correlation with total starch. With increase in non-reducing sugar amylose decreased and glycemic index increased. Total starch had significant positive correlation to amylose and amylopectin while amylose was negatively correlated to glycemic index. Though resistant starch had positive correlation with glycemic index it was not statistically significant. Perusal of Table 12 indicated that soluble dietary fiber was positively and significantly correlated to total and insoluble fiber, while insoluble dietary fiber had significant positive correlation with total dietary fiber and glycemic index. Tannins exhibited significant positive correlation to glycemic index (Table 13).

4.7 VALUE ADDITION TO JACKFRUIT OF DIFFERENT STAGES OF MATURITY

Value addition refers to increasing the value of any food in terms of either nutritive value, sensory quality, health benefits or economic value. Jackfruit at different stages of maturity was converted into flour and therapeutic food mix. The products were evaluated for quality and the results are presented in this section.

4.7.1 Preparation of jackfruit flour at different stages of maturity

Processing, formulation and gaining acceptance of developed food are basic steps of product development. To complete these steps there are several sub-steps required to be performed essentially. Besides organoleptic characteristics, physical and functional properties are equally important. Functional properties of developed food are measured to know the method of handling developed product during end use (Plate 4).

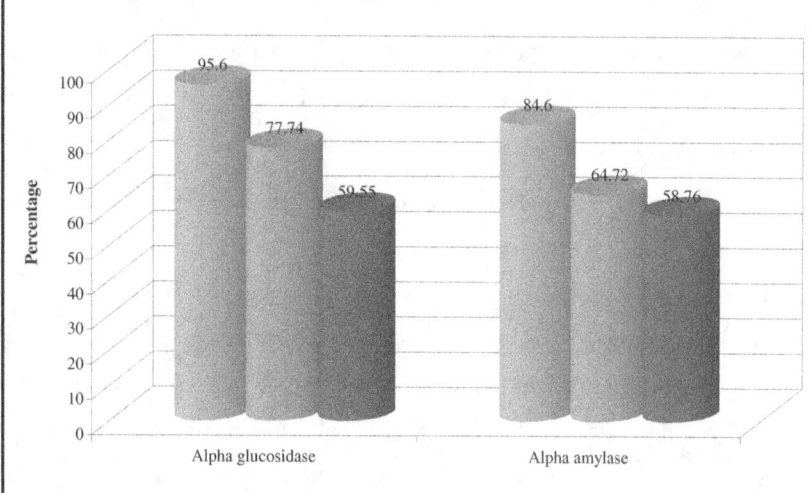

Fig. 8. Anti-diabetic activity of jackfruit at different stages of maturity

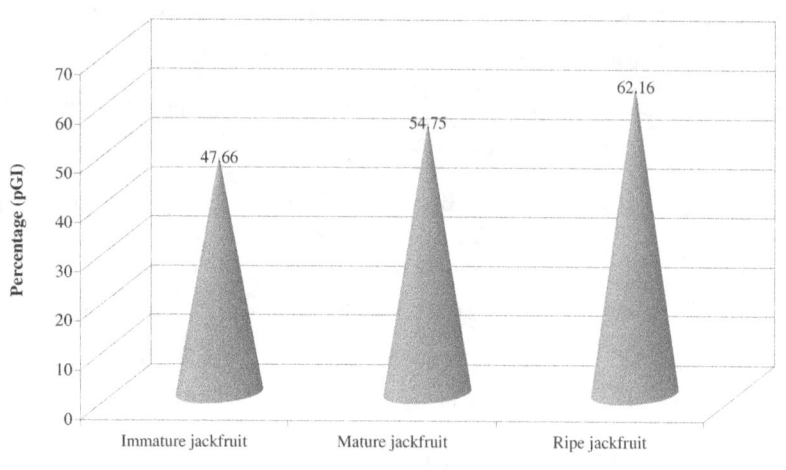

Stages of maturity of jackfruit

Fig. 9. Glycemic index of jackfruit at different stages of maturity

Table 11 Correlation between carbohydrate profile and glycemic index of jackfruit at different stages of maturity

Parameters	TS	RS	NRS	TSt	Amylose	Amylopectin	RS	PGI
Total sugar	1	0.98**	0.98**	-0.76*	-0.95**	-0.47	0.27	0.93**
Reducing Sugar		1	0.95**	-0.85**	0.96**	-0.60	0.13	0.87
Non Reducing Sugar			1	-0.65	-0.92**	-032	0.40	0.98**
Total Starch				1	0.85**	0.92**	0.35	-0.49
Amylose					1	0.58	-0.15	-0.84**
Amylopection						1	0.64	-0.13
Resistant Starch							1	0.56
PGI								1

TSt: Total Starch, RS: Reducing sugar, NRS: Non Reducing Sugar, TS: Total Sugar,
RS: Resistant Starch, pGI: predicted glycemic index
* significant at the 0.05 level; ** significant at the 0.01 level

Table 12: Correlation between dietary fiber and glycemic index of jackfruit at different stages of maturity

Dietary fiber components	SDF	IDF	TDF	PGI
SDF	1	0.79*	0.91**	0.11
IDF		1	0.96**	0.69*
TDF			1	0.50
pGI				1

SDF: soluble dietary fiber, IDF:insoluble dietary fiber, TDF: total dietary fiber, pGI:
predicted glycemic index, *Correlation is significant at the 0.05 level,
** Correlation is significant at the 0.01 level

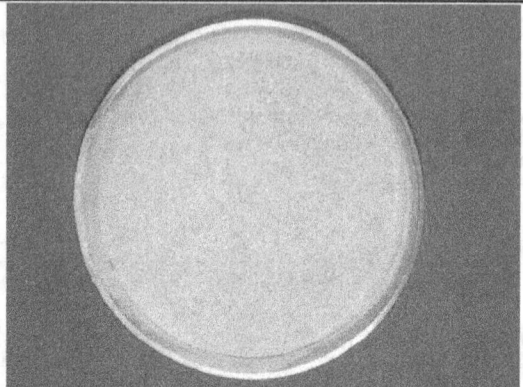

Immature jackfruit flour

Mature jackfruit flour

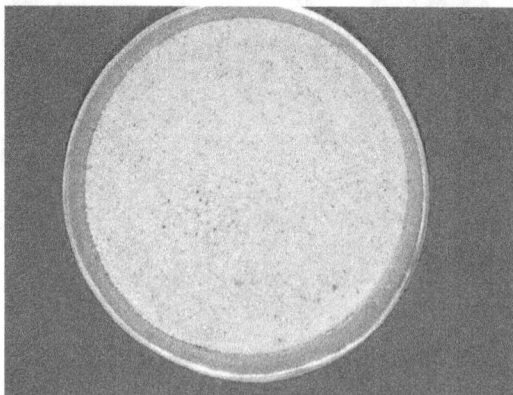

Ripe jackfruit flour

Plate 4. Immature, mature and ripe flour of jackfruit

4.7.1.1 Physical parameter of the jackfruit flour at different stages of maturity

The physical properties include weight, volume, bulk density, colour, particle size and many more.

The physical properties of jackfruit flour at different stages of maturity are presented in Table 14. Total flour yield was 20.00, 26.84 and 19.04 per cent in immature, mature and ripe jackfruit respectively. Flour of jackfruit of all three stages was acidic, with higher pH in mature (6.20) followed by ripe (5.72) and immature (5.71) jackfruit flour. Total titrable acidity was recorded highest in ripe (0.38%) followed by mature (0.26%) and immature (0.17%) jackfruit flour. Bulk density (g/ml) was significantly higher in mature (0.65 g/ml) in comparison to immature jackfruit flour (0.45g/ml). Properties like milling yield and bulk density could not be estimated for ripe flour due to higher hygroscopicity of the flour.

Distribution of particle size (%) of jackfruit flour of different stages of maturity is indicated in Table 15. Higher proportion of immature and mature jackfruit flours were of 180μm (30.05 and 29.67 % respectively), followed by 250 μm (16.86 and 18.77g/100g respectively). Very less per cent of flour was of fine particles having 53 μm (5.02 and 1.28% respectively). The distribution of size of particles differed significantly between immature and mature jackfruits.

Table 16 exhibits the lightness (L*), redness (a*), yellowness (b*), Chroma (C*) of the developed jackfruit flour in different stages of maturity. The flour of mature jackfruit was lighter with L value of 85.86 followed by ripe jackfruit flour (79.30). The immature jackfruit flour was darker with L value of 74.21. Mature jackfruit flour (2.98) showed lower redness compared to ripe (5.83), but higher redness was observed in immature fruit flour (7.21). Both immature and ripe fruit flours had higher yellowness (20.41 and 19.98 respectively), whereas mature fruit flour exhibited lower yellowness (13.10). The L, a, b values of mature jackfruit flour (85.86, 2.98 & 13.10 respectively) were nearer to the values of wheat flour (89.87, 1.47 & 10.92 respectively).

4.7.1.2 Functional properties of jackfruit flour at different stages of maturity

The functional properties of jackfruit flour of different stages of maturity are presented in Table 17. Ripe fruit flour was not analysed for functional properties owing to higher hygroscopicity. Water absorption capacity, oil absorption capacity, swelling capacity

Table 13: Correlation between antioxidant components and glycemic index of jackfruit at different stages of maturity

Parameters	Total Phenols	Tannins	PGI
Total Phenol	1	-0.56	-0.10
Tannins		1	0.87**
PGI			1

** significant at the 0.01 level

Table 14 Physical properties of jackfruit flour at different stages of maturity

Physical properties	Stages of maturity		
	Immature	Mature	Ripe
Yield (%)	20.00	26.84	19.04
pH	5.71	6.20	5.72
TTA (%)	0.17	0.26	0.38
Bulk density (g/ml)	0.45	0.65	–

Note: Bulk density of ripe jackfruit flour could not be estimated due to its hygroscopicity.
TTA: Total Titrable Acidity

Table 14a "t" values for physical properties of jackfruit flour at different stages of maturity

	Immature and mature		Mature and ripe		Immature and ripe	
Physical properties	't' Value	P Value	't' Value	P Value	't' Value	P Value
Yield (%)	7.69*	0.002	8.15*	0.001	0.612	NS
pH	8.32*	0.001	9.29*	0.001	0.51	NS
TTA (%)	6.79*	0.001	1.29	NS	1.29	NS
Bulk density (g/ml)	12.24*	0.00	–	–	–	–

Note: * Significant @5% , NS: Non significant TTA: total titrable acidity

Table 15 Particle size (%) distribution of jackfruit flour at different stages of maturity

Stages of maturity	BSS Standard [Sieve Opening (µm)]						
	60(250)	85(180)	100(150)	150(105)	200(75)	240(63)	300(53)
Immature	16.86±0.01	30.05±0.04	15.03±0.01	10.57±0.21	18.15±0.12	4.54±0.65	0
Mature	18.77±0.01	29.67±0.04	14.40±0.43	20.89±0.01	11.56±0.62	3.50±0.03	0
t-value	170.38*	10.75*	2.08^{NS}	68.80*	14.87*	2.26^{NS}	16.97*
P-value	0.00	0.009	0.17	0.00	0.004	0.152	0.003

Note. Ripe jackfruit flour was not assessed because of its hygroscopicity
Values are the mean of three replications;SEm- Standard Error mean,
CD- Critical Difference, NS- Non Significant, * Significant @5%,

Table 16. Color of jackfruit flour at different stages of maturity

Source	Wheat flour	Immature jackfruit flour	Mature Jackfruit flour	Ripe Jackfruit flour	F value	Sem	CD
L*- Lightness	89.87±0.01	74.21±0.69	85.86±0.03	79.30±0.44	844.27	0.23	0.77*
a*-Redness	1.47±0.04	7.21±0.11	2.98±0.02	5.83±0.03	5961.53	0.03	0.10*
b*- Yellowness	10.92±0.16	20.41± 0.46	13.10±0.09	19.98±0.22	1037.44	0.14	0.48*
C*-Chroma	11.02±0.06	21.65±0.03	13.44±0.04	20.81±0.05	62870.97	0.01	0.05*
H0- Hue	82.28±0.13	70.51±0.06	77.14±0.04	73.7±0.1	200035.23	0.03	0.11*

Values are the mean of three replications;SEm- Standard Error mean,
CD- Critical Difference, NS- Non Significant, * Significant @5%,

and solubility were higher in mature jackfruit flour (308.66%, 19.67%, 8.92% and 17.84% respectively) compared to immature flour (148.82%, 7.00%, 4.23% and 10.04% respectively). Student 't' value indicated significant difference between the two stages of maturity.

Table 18 records the descriptive characteristics of jackfruit flour at the three different stages of maturity *viz.* immature, mature and ripe in terms of colour, odour, taste and texture. It was observed that immature jack flour was brown having strong husky odour, moderately astringent and free flowing in texture. On the other hand, mature jackfruit flour was whitish in color having pleasant roasted aroma, slightly astringent in taste with smooth and free flowing texture. Ripe jackfruit flour was tough to handle and was golden brown in color, carried caramelized odour, sweet in taste and it was too hygroscopic to be sieved.

4.7.2 Development of mature jackfruit based antidiabetic composite mix

Jackfruit flour developed was used to formulate composite mix using other ingredients and evaluated for sensory acceptability, storage quality and health benefits and the results are presented in the section.

Trials with variations in jackfruit flour for formulation of composite mix have been explained in Table 19. Immature jackfruit flour when blended with wheat flour in the ratio of 10:90 was good in taste and could be consumed, but when proportion of jackfruit flour was increased to 20 and 30 per cent, bitterness was pronounced and chapathi was dark brown in colour. The product was unacceptable. Hence could not be continued.

Mature jackfruit flour when combined with wheat flour in the ratio of 10:90, jackfruit was not detectable, texture of chapatti was soft, pliable and acceptable. Formulations in the ratio of 20:80, 30:70, 40:60 was remarked as good in taste, and highly acceptable. Formulation with 50 per cent jack fruit flour with 50 per cent wheat flour was acceptable and good in taste. It was suggested to add spices to mask slight astringent taste felt and to enhance the palatability of chapatti. The composite flour in the ratio of 60:40 was acceptable but astringency was observed, hence, suggested to add spices to mask astringency.

Table 20 indicates the amounts of spices added to composite mixes to enhance palatability and acceptance. After multiple trials and based on feedback of trails, formulations with 30:70, 40:60, 50:50, and 60:40 of jackfruit flour and wheat flour was added with fixed

Table 17 Functional properties of jackfruit flour at different stages of maturity

Functional properties	Stages of maturity		't' Value	P Value
	Immature	Mature		
Water absorption capacity (%)	148.82	308.66	6190.57***	0.00
Oil absorption capacity (%)	7.00	19.67	21.91***	0.00
Swelling capacity (%)	4.23	8.92	256.88***	0.00
Solubility (%)	10.04	17.84	374.70***	0.00

Note: *** Significant @0.1%,

Table 18 Descriptive characteristics of jackfruit flour

Stages of maturity	Descriptive characteristics
Immature	Brown, Strong husky, Moderately astringent, Free flowing
Mature	White, Roasted aroma, Slightly astringent, Smooth free flowing
Ripe	Chocolate brown, Caramelized odour, Sweet, Highly hygroscopic could not be sieved

Table 19   Standardization of antidiabetic composite mix with variations of jackfruit flour

Trials	Jackfruit flour	Wheat flour	Remarks
Immature jackfruit flour			
I	10	90	Can be consumed
II	20	80	Bitter in taste, cannot be consumed
III	30	70	Dark brown, Bitter in taste, not Acceptable
Mature jackfruit flour			
I	10	90	Jackfruit flour was undetected. Soft, pliable, acceptable chapathi
II	20	80	Good in taste
III	30	70	Good in taste
IV	40	60	Good in taste, acceptable
V	50	50	Acceptable and good in taste. Suggested to add spices
VI	60	40	Acceptable but astringent in taste. Suggested to add spices

amount of spices. Coriander leaves (dried and crushed), dried and crushed green chilli and pepper powder, coriander seed powder and cumin seeds were added. The composite mix was converted to chapatti and tested for sensory quality. It was found out that 30:70, 40:60 and 50:50 ratio mixes were good in taste and texture, soft pliable and good in texture. Formulation of 60:40 ratio was having after taste which persisted for longer duration but texture was good (Plate 5).

4.7.2.1 Sensory scores of chapathi of composite mix from mature jackfruit flour

Descriptive characteristics of dough and chapathi of mature jackfruit flour based composite mix is presented in Table 21 (Plate 6). Around 130ml of luke warm water (40°C) was required to make dough. Elasticity of dough was very low, it was putty and difficult to handle. Rolling of chappati was difficult with rolling pin but flattening with hand was easy and employed. Chapatti took one minute to bake on each side, during which time five to eight brown spots appeared. Thickness of chappati was recorded to be 0.5mm. Cooked chapathi was reported to be edible with acceptable characteristics for 32 hours at room temperature and 72 hours in refrigerator, however, the colour turned darker. After cooling, texture of chapatti was soft, easily foldable and easy to chew. Color of the chapathi after cooking and cooling turned darker with progress of time.

Table 22 shows mean sensory scores of chapathi prepared with mature jackfruit flour based composite mix. Control chapathi prepared with 100 per cent wheat flour received significantly higher scores for all sensory parameters evaluated except flavour. The composite flour having 30 per cent of mature jackfruit flour was scored on par with control with respect to appearance, colour and overall acceptability. Surprisingly flavour of 30:70 chapathi was scored significantly higher than control. With increase in the proportion of mature jackfruit flour, sensory scores decreased. The chapathi prepared with 60:40 ratio of mature jackfruit flour and wheat flour received significantly lower unacceptable scores though the appearance, colour, flavour, taste and texture were scored between 6 and 7, overall it received lower acceptability.

Fig 10 depicts acceptability indices of mature jackfruit flour based composite mix. Highest acceptability index was observed for chapathi of 30:70 mature jackfruit flour based composite mix (89.22%) followed by control- wheat flour chapatti (88.62%). Though other

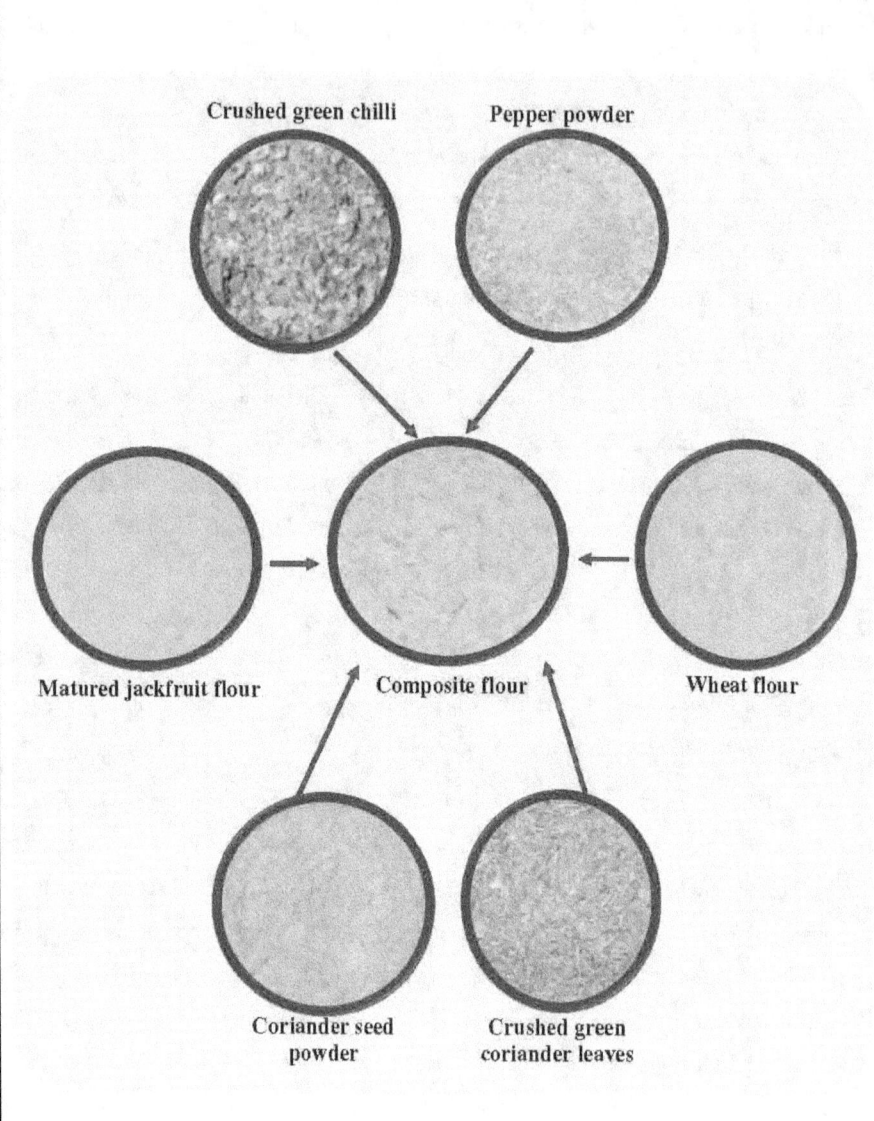

Plate 5. Formulation of composite flour

Table 20 Optimization of mature jackfruit flour based antidiabetic composite mix

Ingredients	Quantity (g)			
Mature jackfruit flour	30	40	50	60
Wheat flour	70	60	50	40
Dried coriander leaves	06	06	06	06
Dried green chilli	0.5	0.5	0.5	0.5
Pepper powder	0.5	0.5	0.5	0.5
Coriander powder	01	01	01	01
Cumin seeds	01	01	01	01
Comments	Good in taste and texture	Good in taste, acceptable, soft pliable	Acceptable, Good in taste and texture	After taste persists longer, Texture is good

Table 21 Descriptive characteristics of dough and chapathi of mature jackfruit flour based composite mix

Parameters	Characteristics
Amount of water required for making dough	130 ml/100g
Elasticity of dough	Very low, dough was putty and difficult to handle
Rolling into chapathi	Difficult to roll out using pin, flattening with hand is recommended
Time of cooking	one min each side
Appearance of brown spots on chapathi	Five to eight spots on both sides
Thickness	0.5 mm
Shelflife of chapathi	24 to 36 hours in normal room temperature and 72 hours in refrigeration
Texture of chapathi after cooling	Soft, easily foldable and easy to chew
Color of product after cooking and cooling	Turns darker with increase in time

Composite mixed flour

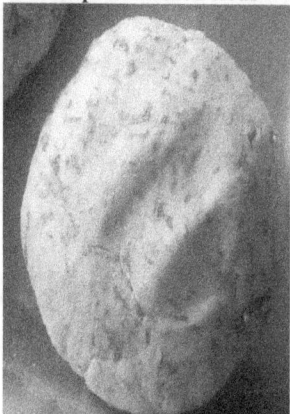

Composite mixed dough

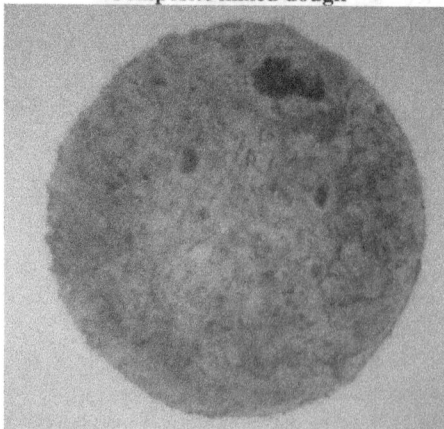

Composite mixed chapathi

Plate 6. Chapathi prepared using antidiabetic composite mix

Table 22 Sensory quality of mature jackfruit flour based composite mix chapathi

Composite flour (MJF:WF)	Appearance	Colour	Flavour	Taste	Texture	Overall acceptability
0.100	8.23±0.71[a]	8.32±0.67[a]	7.73±0.63[b]	7.77±0.81[a]	7.86±0.77[a]	7.95±0.72[a]
30:70	8.09±0.81[a]	8.50±0.5[a]	8.77±0.42[a]	7.18±0.53[b]	7.14±0.83[b]	8.50±0.67[a]
40:60	7.14±0.27[b]	7.07±0.8[b]	7.03±0.67[b]	6.98±0.21[b]	7.51±0.31[a]	7.19±0.07[b]
50:50	7.82±0.78[b]	7.73±0.72[b]	7.05±0.95[b]	7.18±0.8[b]	7.50±0.80[a]	7.36±0.50[h]
60:40	6.18±0.36[c]	6.41±0.45[c]	6.77±0.19[c]	6.68±0.2[c]	7.00±0.75[b]	5.91±0.15[c]
F value	19.27	27.47	25.72	3.21	5.26	36.73
SEm	0.84	0.81	1.17	0.78	0.86	1.72
CD	1.18**	1.15**	1.65**	1.10**	1.22**	2.42**

Sensory evaluation done by nine point hedonic scale, NS- Non Significant, * Significant @5%,
Values with same superscript (a, b) in same columns are not significantly different (P≤0.01)

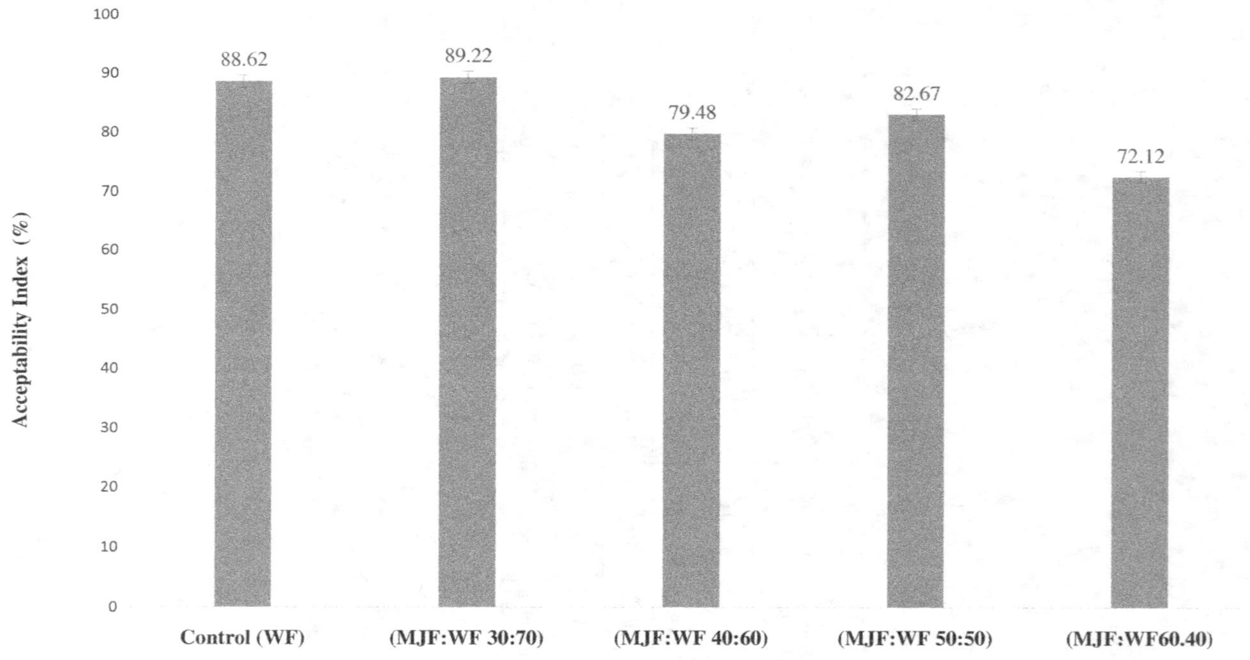

Fig 10 Acceptability index of mature jackfruit flour based composite mix chapathi

formulations (40:60, 50:50, 60:40) received lower acceptability indices, all composite mixes were in acceptable range (79.48, 82.67 and 72.12 % respectively). On the basis of acceptability scores it was decided to continue further studies with 50:50 formulation of mature jackfruit flour and wheat flour.

4.7.2.2 Physical parameters of antidiabetic composite mix

Table 23 exhibits the lightness (L*), redness (a*), yellowness (b*), chroma (C*) of the developed antidiabetic composite mix and chapathi in comparison to wheat flour and wheat chapathi. Composite mix exhibited 'L', 'a', 'b' values of 85.88, 1.97 and 11.92 indicating that composite mix was significantly darker than wheat flour (L-89.87). However, redness and yellowness were lower than mature jackfruit flour ('a'-2.98 and 'b'-13.10). The colour of composite flour chapathi was darker having 'L' value of 44.69 while that of wheat chapathi was 60.87. Redness as indicated by 'a' was higher in wheat chapathi compared to composite mix chapathi (3.47 & 2.52 respectively). Similarly the yellowness was less in composite mix chapathi (9.10) compared to wheat chapathi (14.92). The lightness, redness and yellowness of wheat flour and composite flour differed significantly (Table 23a). Though redness and yellowness of mature jackfruit flour and composite mix differed the lightness was similar. Regarding chapathi of composite mix and wheat flour the lightness, redness and yellowness differed significantly.

The particle size distribution of developed composite mix in comparison to mature jackfruit flour and wheat flour is indicated in Table 24. Higher proportion (41.88%) jackfruit based composite mix passed through 85(180μm) mesh BSS standard sieve, followed by 150 (16.76%) and 60 (15.10%). Very less amount of finer flour was observed having particle size of 63 (2.33%) and 53 (0.73%) microns. Similar trend was observed for wheat flour and mature jackfruit flour. Majority of the particles in mature jackfruit flour and wheat flour were distributed between 250, 180, 150 and 105 microns (18.77, 29.66, 14.39, 20.89% and 26.05, 30.03, 27.08, 11.72% respectively). Very less quantity of all three types of flour were of finer particles which passed through 240 and 300 mesh size.

4.7.2.3 Functional properties of antidiabetic composite mix

Functional properties include capacity to swell, absorb water, oil and alike. The results of functional properties of antidiabetic composite mix in comparison to mature

Table 23 Color assessment of flours and chapathi of jackfruit based composite mix

Source	Flours			Chapathi	
	Wheat flour	Mature jackfruit flour	Composite Mix	Wheat (control)	Composite Mix
L*- Lightness	89.87±0.01	85.86±003	85.88±0.02	60.87±0.05	44.69±0.05
a*-Redness	1.47±0.04	2.98±0.02	1.97±0.01	3.47±0.07	2.52±0.06
b*-Yellowness	10.92±0.16	13.08±0.09	11.92±0.02	14.92±0.12	9.10±0.01
C*-Chroma	11.02±0.06	13.44±0.04	12.08±0.04	14.02±0.03	9.44±0.06
H^{0-} Hue	82.28±0.13	77.14±0.04	80.58±0.05	89.28±0.06	74.47±0.17

Table 23a Comparison between color of diferent flours and chapathis of jackfruit based composite mix

Source	Flours						Chapathi	
	WF and MJF		MJF and CM		WF and CM		WC and CMC	
	t value	P value	t value	P value	t value	P value	t value	P value
L*- Lightness	206.48	0.000	0.96	NS	83.48	.000	1035.08	.000
a*-Redness	88.84	0.001	62.97	.000	45.39	.000	31.30	.000
b*-Yellowness	41.33	0.000	21.74	.000	192.38	.000	103.72	.000
C*-Chroma	103.85	0.000	41.22	.000	48.23	.000	972.97	.000
H0- Hue	222.56	0.000	139.29	.000	31.30	.000	634.85	.000

Where WF: wheat flour, MJF: mature jackfruit flour, CM: composite mix, WC: wheat chapathi, CMC: composite mix chapathi

jackfruit flour and wheat flour are presented in Table 25. Water absorption capacity of composite mix (199.46%) was significantly lower than that of mature jackfruit flour (308.66%) and significantly higher than wheat flour (66.40). On the contrary, oil absorption capacity of composite mix (308.23%) was significantly higher than mature jackfruit flour (19.67%) and was on par with that of wheat flour (310.77%). Swelling capacity of composite mix (49.70%) was significantly higher than that of wheat flour (3.10%) and mature jackfruit flour (8.92%). The solubility of composite mix was 11.93 per cent which was significantly lower than that of wheat flour (9.24%) and significantly higher than mature jackfruit flour (17.83%).

4.7.2.4 Proximate composition of antidiabetic composite mix

Table 26 shows the proximate composition of developed composite mix. Moisture, crude fat and ash contents of composite mix (8.26, 1.72 and 2.45% respectively) were significantly lower than in mature jackfruit flour (8.29, 2.43 and 7.16% respectively). Protein, crude fiber, total and available carbohydrate (13.68, 5.08, 73.89 and 68.81%) were significantly higher in composite mix compared to mature jackfruit flour (4.36, 3.53, 81.43 and 74.33% respectively). Mature jackfruit flour contained significantly higher energy of 365 kcal while it was 346 kcal in antidiabetic composite mix.

4.7.2.5 Nutritional quality of antidiabetic composite mix

Nutritional quality of antidiabetic composite mix was estimated in terms of IVPD and IVSD and results are shown in Fig 11 and Table 27. Figure 11 depicts *in-vitro* protein digestibility of developed composite mix. Composite mix exhibited 88 per cent of protein digestibility which was significantly lower than that of mature jackfruit flour (92%).

Starch digestibility of antidiabetic composite mix (Table 27) was observed to be highest at 90 min (11.53%) followed by 120 min (10.98%) and lower at 30 min (6.89%). The digestibility in mature jackfruit flour was highest (19.35%) at 120 min followed by 90 (12.76%) and 30 min (12.53%). The mature jackfruit flour and developed antidiabetic composite mix differed significantly as indicated by 't' test.

Starch digestibility index was recorded higher (30.93) in composite flour compared to mature jackfruit flour (27.84) as shown in figure 12.

Table 24 Particle size distribution (%) of developed composite mix

Flour sample	BSS Standard [Sieve Opening (μm)]						
	60(250)	85(180)	100(150)	150(105)	200(75)	240(63)	300(53)
MJF	18.77 ± 0.01[b]	29.66 ±0.04[b]	14.39 ±0.43[b]	20.89 ±0.01[a]	11.55 ±0.62[a]	3.50 ±0.03[a]	1.28 ±0.31[a]
Wheat flour	26.05 ± 1.3[a]	30.03 ±1.77[b]	27.08 ±0.01[a]	11.72 ±0.01[c]	4.12 ±0.001[b]	2.09 ±0.00[b]	0.01 ±0.00[b]
Composite flour	15.10 ± 1.29[c]	41.88 ±0.28[a]	12.43 ±0.28[c]	16.76 ±0.04[b]	10.86 ±0.31[a]	2.33 ±0.48[b]	0.73 ±0.04[a]
F Value	111.41	89.64	1426.78	66748.76	212.60	14.72	24.68
SEm	0.43	0.60	0.17	0.02	0.23	0.16	0.10
CD	1.94**	2.70**	0.78**	0.08**	1.03**	0.72*	0.47*

MJF: Mature Jackfruit Flour; *Significant @5%, ** Significant @0.01%, Values with same superscript (a, b, c) in same columns are not significantly different (P≤0.01).) Values are the mean of three replications; SEm- Standard Error mean, CD- Critical Difference.

Table 25 Functional properties of antidiabetic composite mix

Functional properties (%)	Mature Jackfruit flour	Wheat Flour	Composite mix	F value	SEM	CD
Water absorption capacity	308.66±0.65[a]	66.40±1.5[c]	199.46±0.23[b]	1000.72	3.84	2.22*
Oil absorption capacity	19.67±0.35[c]	310.77±1.2[a]	308.23±2.7[b]	286.12	9.89	5.72*
Swelling capacity	8.92±0.10[b]	3.10±0.12[c]	49.70±0.8[a]	0.89	26.89	15.54*
Solubility	17.83±0.00[a]	9.24±0.23[c]	11.93±0.44[b]	8.09	1.55	0.89*

* Significant @5%, values with same superscript (a, b) in same columns are not significantly different (P≤0.01)

Table 26 Proximate composition (dwb) of developed composite mix

Proximate Composition (%)	Composite mix	Mature jackfruit flour	't' Value	P Value
Moisture	8.26±0.33	8.29±1.24	0.04*	0.966
Protein	13.68±0.67	4.36±0.6	23.767*	0.000
Crude Fat	1.72±0.18	2.43±0.04	6.44*	0.003
Crude fiber	5.08±0.78	7.16±0.03	33.147*	0.000
Ash	2.45±0.5	3.53±0.01	51.88*	0.000
Total Carbohydrate	73.89± 0.05	81.43±0.08	763.13*	0.000
Available Carbohydrate	68.81±0.51	74.33±0.03	613.58*	0.000
Energy (kcal)	346	365	4374.4*	0.000

Note: *Significant @5%

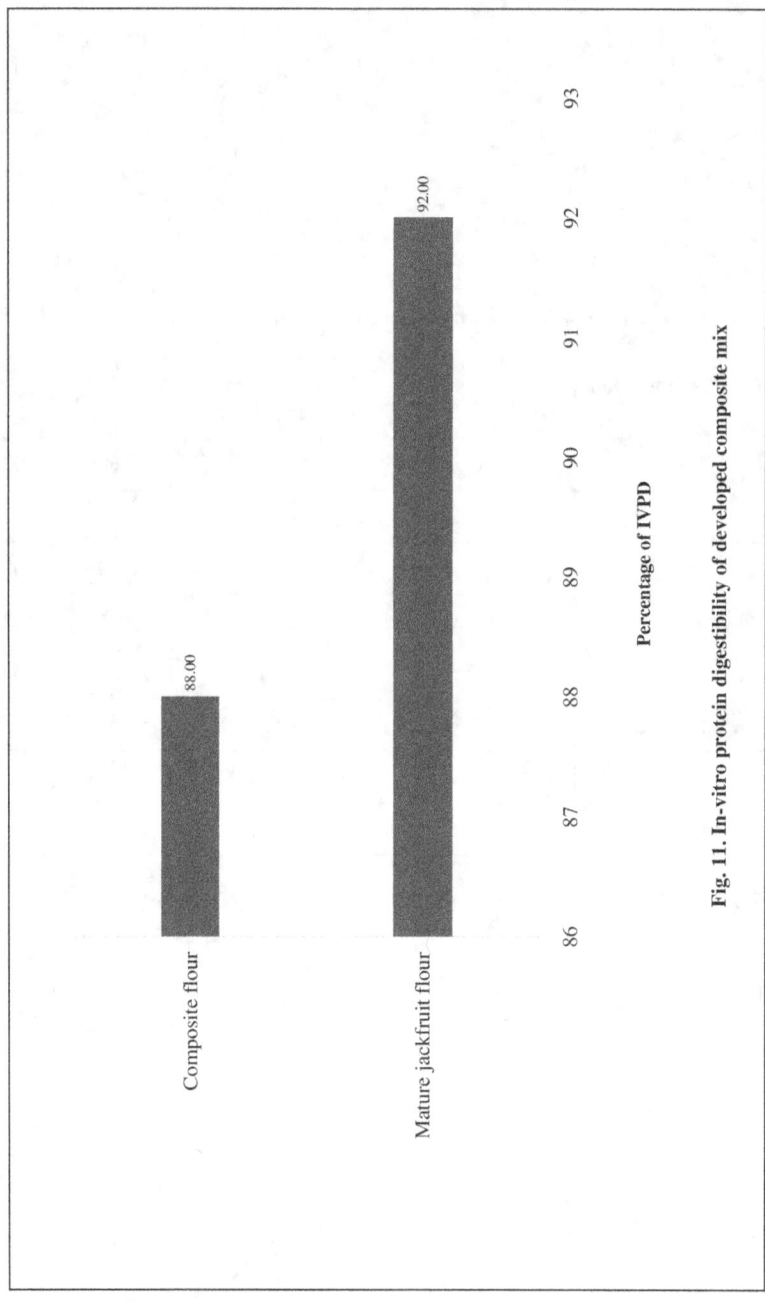

Fig. 11. In-vitro protein digestibility of developed composite mix

Table 27. *In-vitro* starch digestibility of jackfruit based composite mix

Sample	*In-vitro* starch digestibility (%)		
	30 min	90 min	120 min
Composite mix	6.89±.39	11.53±.58	10.98±.25
Mature jackfruit	12.53±.040	12.76±.030	19.35±.030
't' Value	24.39**	3.657**	56.826**
P Value	0.02	0.22	0.00

** significant at 1% level

4.7.2.6 Antioxidant components and activity of antidiabetic composite mix

Dietary fibre, tannins and polyphenols represent antioxidant components. Fig 13 represents dietary fibre content of composite mix in comparison to mature jackfruit flour. Soluble, insoluble and total dietary fibre was recorded to be significantly higher in composite mix (7.16, 14.70 and 21.68% respectively) compared to mature jackfruit flour (5.00, 9.70 and 14.70% respectively).

Table 28 expresses antioxidant components present in composite mix. Composite flour contained significantly higher amounts of polyphenols and tannins compared to mature jackfruit flour. The values of polyphenols were 90.16 mg GAE/g and 53.10 mg GAE/g for antidiabetic composite flour and mature jackfruit flour respectively. Similarly, higher amounts of tannins were observed in composite mix (89.40 mgTAE/g), while in mature jackfruit flour it was in traces (0.41 mgTAE/g). The antioxidant activity in terms of DPPH scavenging was significantly higher in composite mix (96.00%) compared to mature jackfruit flour (79.00 %). Similarly, phosphomolybdenum inhibition was also significantly higher in composite mix (79.00%) compared to mature jackfruit flour (61.43%).

4.8 STORAGE QUALITY OF DEVELOPED ANTIDIABETIC COMPOSITE MIX

Antidiabetic composite mix was packed in polyethylene and aluminium foil coated pouches and stored at ambient temperature for a period of six months (plate 7). Analysis of sensory, chemical and microbial quality was carried out periodically and results are presented in this section.

4.8.1 Effect of storage on moisture content of developed composite mix

Effect of storage on moisture content of developed composite mix is shown in Table 29. It was observed that with the increase in storage period, there was an increase in moisture content in both the packaging material. When freshly made the moisture content was 8.24 per cent which increased to 11.23 per cent in high density polyethylene and to 10.72 per cent in aluminium foil coated pouches, at the end of storage (180 day) period. Though there was numerical increase in moisture content, it was statistically not significant. The packaging material and duration of storage did not influence the moisture content of the developed mix.

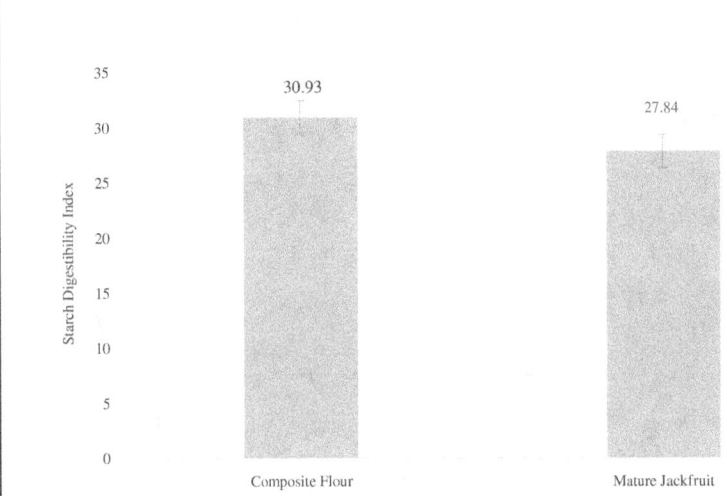

Fig. 12. Starch digestibility index of mature jackfruit flour based composite mix

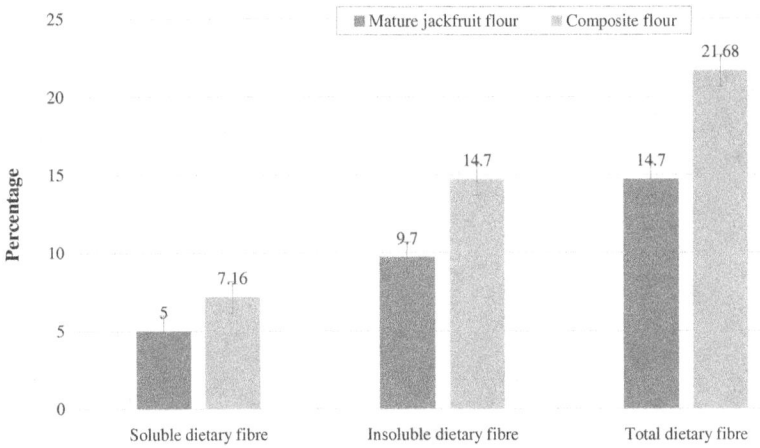

Components of dietary fibre

Fig. 13. Dietary fibre content of developed composite mix

Table 28 Antioxidant component and activity of jackfruit based composite mix

Parameters	Composite mix	Mature jackfruit flour	't' Value	P Value
Antioxidant components				
Polyphenols (mg GAE/g)	90.16±0.05	53.10±2.7	22.93*	0.00
Tannins (mg TAE/g)	89.40±0.2	0.41±0.17	573.854*	0.00
Antioxidant activity (%)				
DPPH	96.00±2.00	67.41±00	23.97*	0.00
Phosphomolybdenum	79.00±2.00	61.43±0.57	15.21*	0.00

Note: * Significant @ 5%, values are mean of three replications

Table 29 Effect of storage on moisture content of developed composite mix

Days of storage	Packaging material	
	HDPE	ALPE
0	8.24	8.24
15	8.62	8.31
30	8.72	8.56
45	9.24	8.92
60	9.44	9.35
75	9.57	9.35
90	9.69	9.39
105	9.68	9.78
120	9.92	9.93
135	9.95	9.96
150	10.25	10.08
165	11.14	10.44
180	11.23	10.72
	F Value	**S.Em.**	**CD**
Packaging material - A	0.206	1.460	NS
Storage days - B	0.966	0.572	NS
Interaction (A×B)	0.018	0.405	NS

Note: Values are mean of three replications, stored at ambient temperature

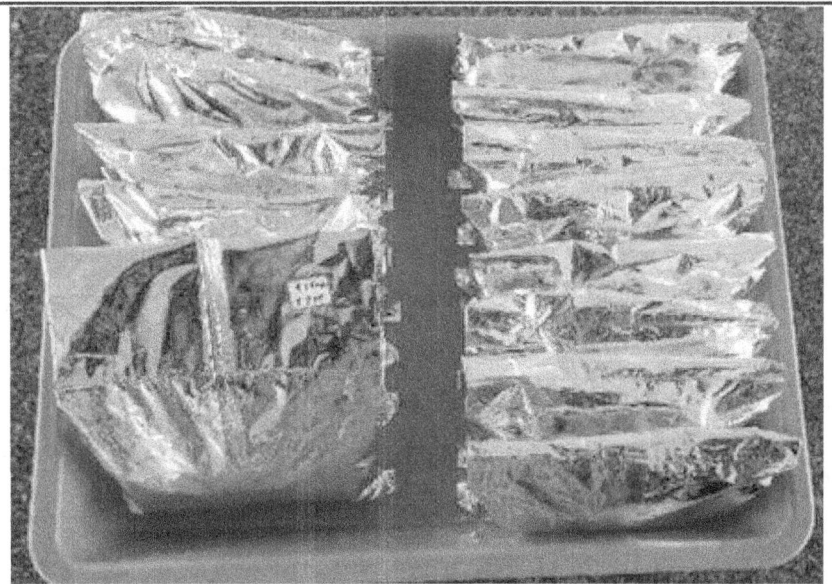

Aluminium coated pouches packaging

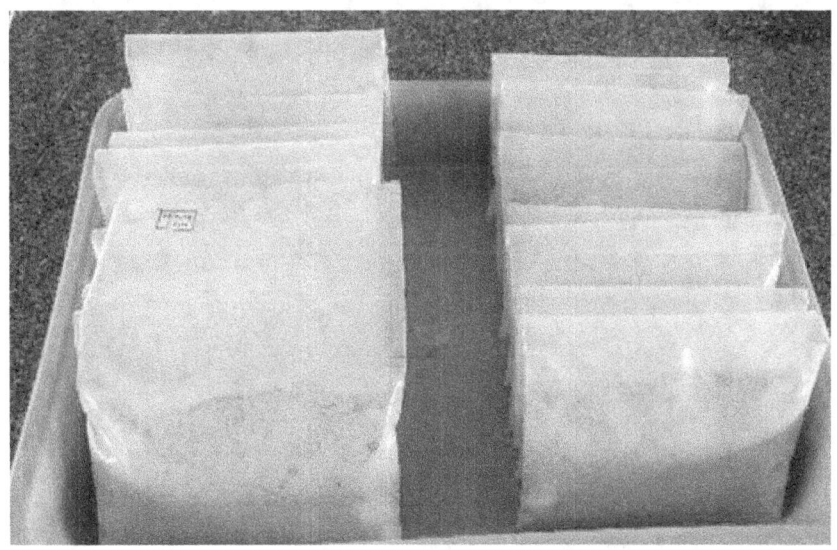

High density polyethylene packets

Plate 7. Storage of anti-diabetic composite mix at ambient temperature

Percent increase in moisture over initial is depicted in Fig 14. Trend of increase in moisture was slightly higher in high density polyethylene package till 120th day (15.15%) in comparison to aluminium foil coated pouches (12.30%). After 120th day both the packaging materials showed similar rise till 165th day (17.18 to 22%). In last 15 days higher increase of moisture observed in both packaging material. At 180th day, the high density polyethylene package showed 28.29 per cent increase whereas aluminium foil coated pouches showed 21.83 per cent. However, the increase in moisture content was within permissible limit.

4.8.2 Effect of storage on sensory parameters of developed composite mix

Figure 15, 16, Table 30 indicates sensory quality of developed composite mix during storage period. The appearance, colour and texture were affected significantly with packaging material but days of storage did not influence these parameters. Appearance of composite mix at zero day was recorded to be 8.33 and at the end of storage period (180th day) it was 8.38 and 7.50 in aluminium foil pouches and high density polyethylene respectively. The color of composite mix was scored 8.17 when freshly prepared which decreased to 8.00 in aluminium foil package and to 7.76 in high density polyethylene pouches at the end of the storage period. Texture of *chapathi* of antidiabetic composite mix enhanced significantly from 7.52 to 7.58 and 7.33 in aluminium foil and HDPE packages respectively. It was noteworthy that the flavour, taste and overall acceptability were not affected by the storage period. The three parameters were scored between like moderately to like very much.

The acceptability indices (Fig 16) of *chapathi* of developed composite mix were higher after 75, 105 and 135 days of storage. However, the indices during storage period ranged between 80 and 90, indicating highly acceptable scores.

4.8.3 Effect of storage on antioxidant activity of developed composite mix

Table 31 indicates the effect of storage on antioxidant activity of developed composite mix. DPPH (2,2-diphenyl-1-picryl-hydrazyl-hydrate) inhibition was 96 per cent at the beginning of storage period which reduced to 85.76 and 86.45 per cent after 180th day of storage in aluminium foil and high density polyethylene packages respectively. Total antioxidant capacity (TAC) was 79 per cent at the beginning of storage when fresh which decreased to 63.57 and 63.51 respectively in aluminium foil and HDPE packages at the end

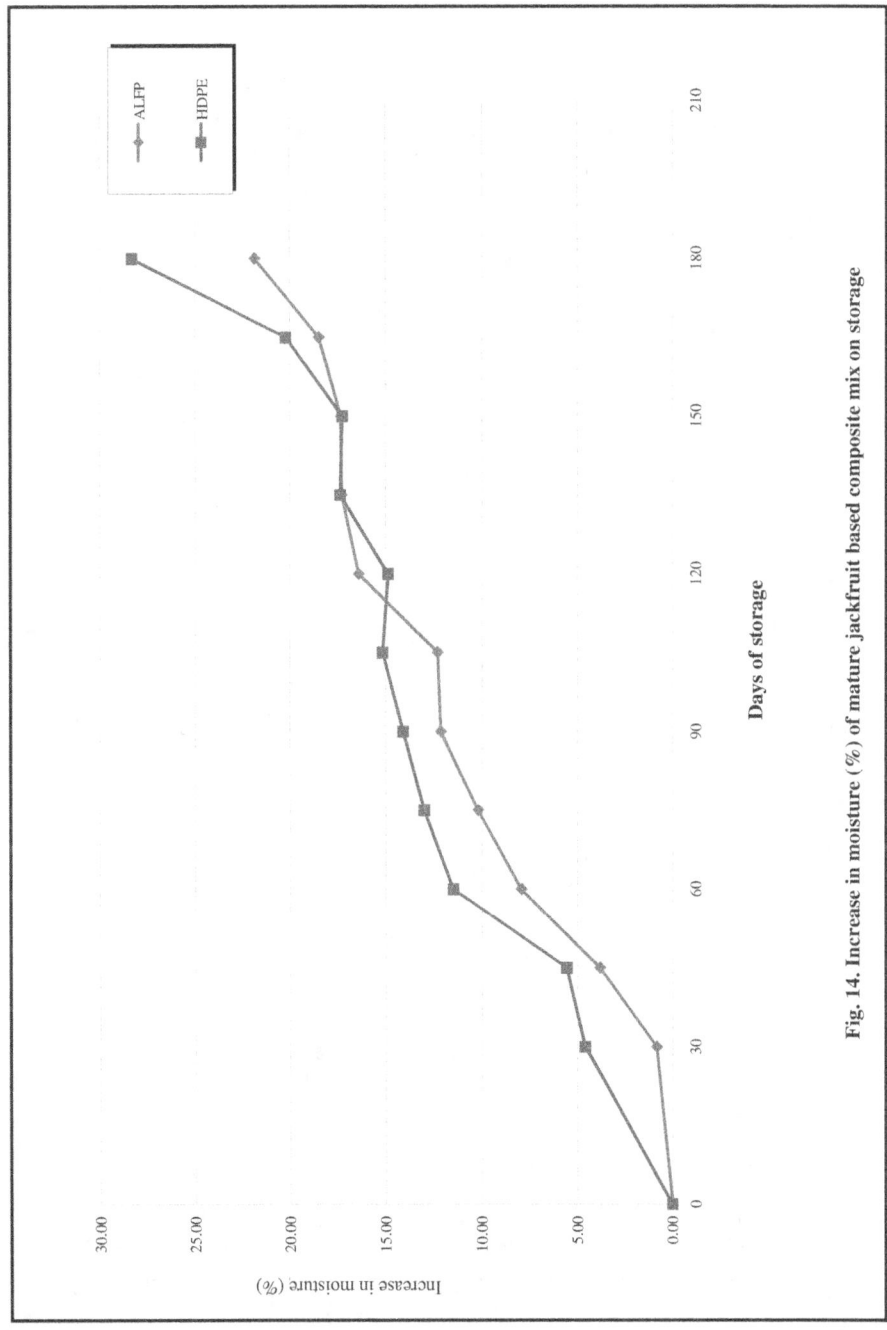

Fig. 14. Increase in moisture (%) of mature jackfruit based composite mix on storage

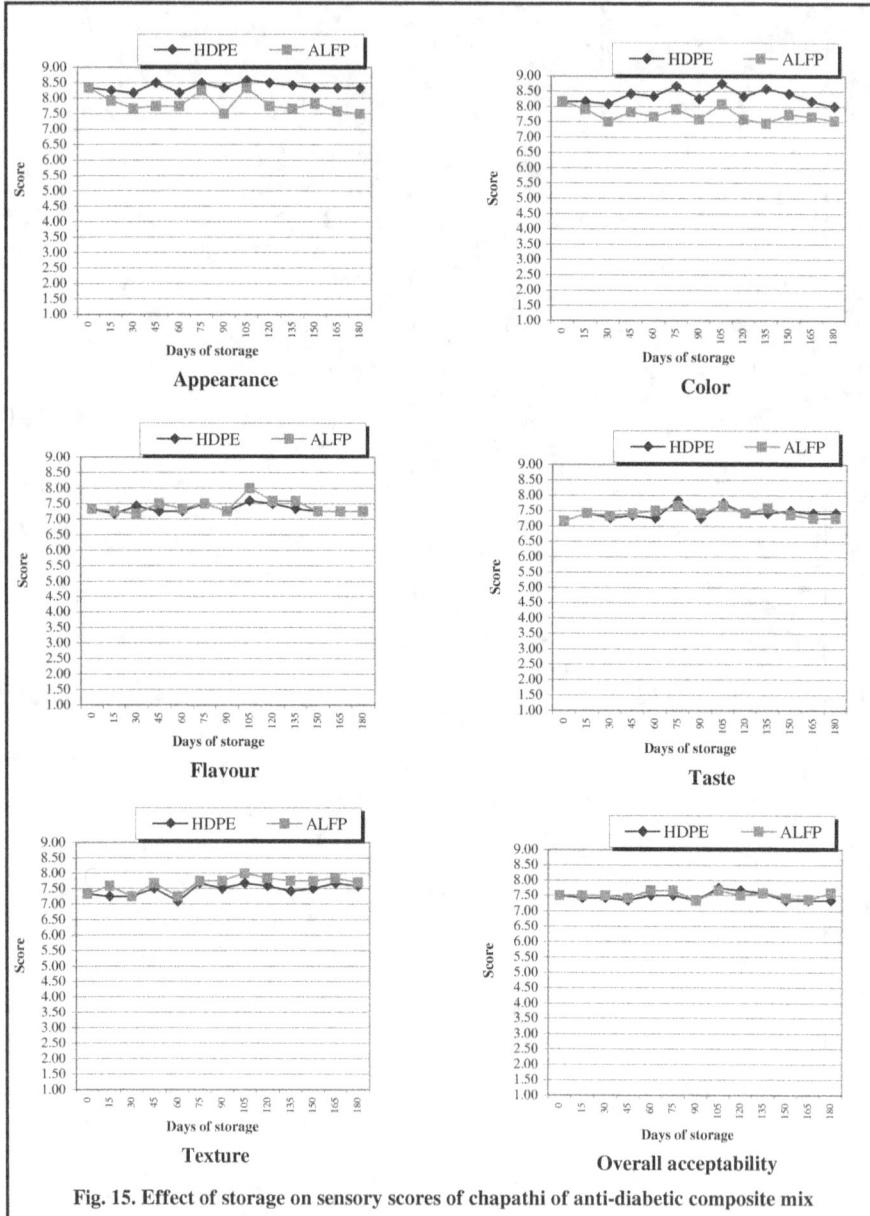

Fig. 15. Effect of storage on sensory scores of chapathi of anti-diabetic composite mix

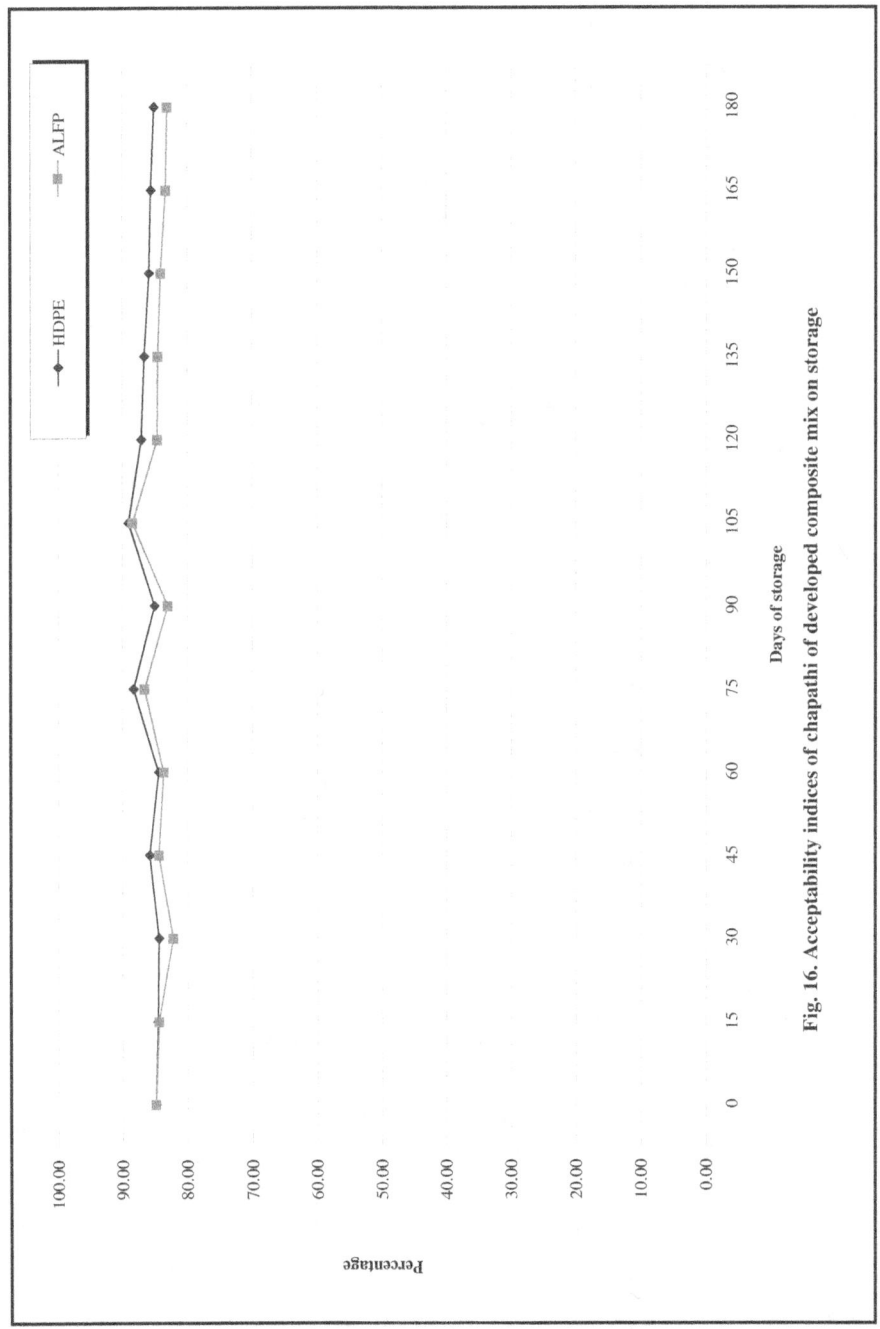

Fig. 16. Acceptability indices of chapathi of developed composite mix on storage

Table 30 Analysis of Variance of sensory scores of developed composite mix chapathi on storage

Source	Appearance			Color			Flavour			Taste			Texture			Overall Acceptability		
	F value	SEm	CD	F value	SEm	CD	F value	SEm	CD	F value	SEm	CD	F value	SEm	CD	F value	SEm	CD
A=Package	41.29	0.51	1.43*	53.83	0.5	1.39*	0.48	0.63	NS	0	0.49	NS	4.85	0.53	1.49*	0.52	0.47	NS
B=Days	1.51	0.2	NS	1.6	0.19	NS	0.81	0.24	NS	1.22	0.19	NS	1.72	0.21	NS	0.69	0.18	NS
AxB	0.81	0.14	NS	0.84	0.13	NS	0.19	0.17	NS	0.23	0.13	NS	0.14	0.14	NS	0.16	0.13	NS

Note: * significant 0.05; Values are mean of three replications

of storage. Nonetheless, these decreases were statistically on par with each other. The packaging material did not influence the antioxidant capacity and activity of the mature jackfruit based antidiabetic composite mix.

Table 31a shows decrease in antioxidant activity of developed composite mix during storage. No change was observed at 30th day in both the packaging material in case of DPPH inhibition, whereas slight change (1.04% and 2.05%) was observed in phosphomolybdenum inhibition at 30th day in both the packaging. DPPH Inhibition reduced suddenly by 9.41 per cent after 150 days of storage whereas a sharp decrease of 8.92 per cent was observed after at 90th days. The packaging material did not influence reduction in antioxidant activity of composite mix.

4.8.4 Effect of storage on microbial quality of developed composite mix

Storage results in many changes in chemical composition, sensory quality, besides changes in microbial load. The results of microbial quality of antidiabetic composite mix on storage are indicated in Table 32. With increase in storage period, load of both bacteria and fungi increased considerably. When freshly prepared only one colony of bacteria was detected in the mix, it increased to 2.72×10^2 and 2.67×10^2 CFU/g in aluminium foil and high density polyethylene packages respectively after 180 days of storage. The increase was higher in aluminium foil package compared to HDPE. Similarly the fungal count were not detected when freshly prepared but increased to 8.25×10^1 and 8.45×10^1 CFU/g at the end of storage period upto 180 days. It was noticeable that E. coli was not present even after 180 days and Actinomycetes were not detected at 0 days of storage in both packaging materials tested, thus its testing was discontinued for further. However, the increase in bacterial and fungal count was within permissible limit (Plate 8).

4.9 EFFICACY OF THE DEVELOPED ANTIDIABETIC MIX IN CONTROLLING BLOOD GLUCOSE

Developed antidiabetic mix was evaluated for antidiabetic property in terms of alpha amylase inhibition, alpha glucosidase inhibition and glycemic index by *in vitro* method. *In vivo* glycemic index was tested for developed mix converting into *chapathi* and feeding non-diabetics volunteers. The results are presented in this section.

Table 31 Effect of storage on antioxidant activity (%) of developed composite mix

DAYS	DPPH			TAC		
	ALFP	HDPE	Mean	ALFP	HDPE	Mean
0	96.00	96.00	96.00	79.00	79.00	79.00
30	96.00	96.00	96.00	78.18	77.38	77.78
60	92.45	92.87	92.66	76.77	76.72	76.75
90	92.32	93.01	92.67	71.95	72.81	72.38
120	90.17	90.32	90.25	70.51	70.41	70.46
150	86.97	89.56	88.27	68.82	69.42	69.12
180	85.76	86.45	86.11	63.57	63.51	63.54
Mean	91.38	92.03	91.71	72.69	72.75	72.72

DPPH	Fvalue	SEM	CD	TAC	Fvalue	SEM	CD
Days	41.01	0.53	1.53*	Days	166.76	0.4	1.17*
Package	3.31	0.99	NS	Package	1.12	0.76	NS
Interaction	0.5	0.37	NS	Interaction	0.7	0.28	NS

Note: DPPH: 2, 2-diphenyl-1-picrylhydrazyl, TAC: total antioxidant capacity, * Significant @5% NS: not significant

Table 31a: Decrease (%) in antioxidant activity of developed composite mix during storage

DAYS	DPPH		TAC	
	ALFP	HDPE	ALFP	HDPE
30	0	0	1.04	2.05
60	3.70	3.26	2.82	2.82
90	3.83	3.12	8.92	7.84
120	3.99	5.92	10.75	10.87
150	9.41	6.71	12.89	12.13
180	10.67	9.95	19.53	19.61
Mean	4.81	4.14	7.99	7.99

Table 32 Effect of storage on microbial quality of developed composite mix

DAYS	Bacterial count (X10^1)		Fungal count (X10^1)		E coli count (X10^1)		Actinomycetes count (X10^1)	
	ALFP	HDPE	ALFP	HDPE	ALFP	HDPE	ALFP	HDPE
0	1	1	0	0	0	0	0	0
30	4.50	4.65	2.00	1.75	0	0	-	-
60	8.76	7.66	3.45	5.00	0	0	-	-
90	12.34	11.65	6.60	7.50	0	0	-	-
120	18.55	17.83	6.45	7.70	0	0	-	-
150	23.40	23.65	8.00	8.50	0	0	-	-
180	27.20	26.76	8.25	8.45	0	0	-	-
MEAN	13.67	13.31	4.96	5.55	-	-	-	-

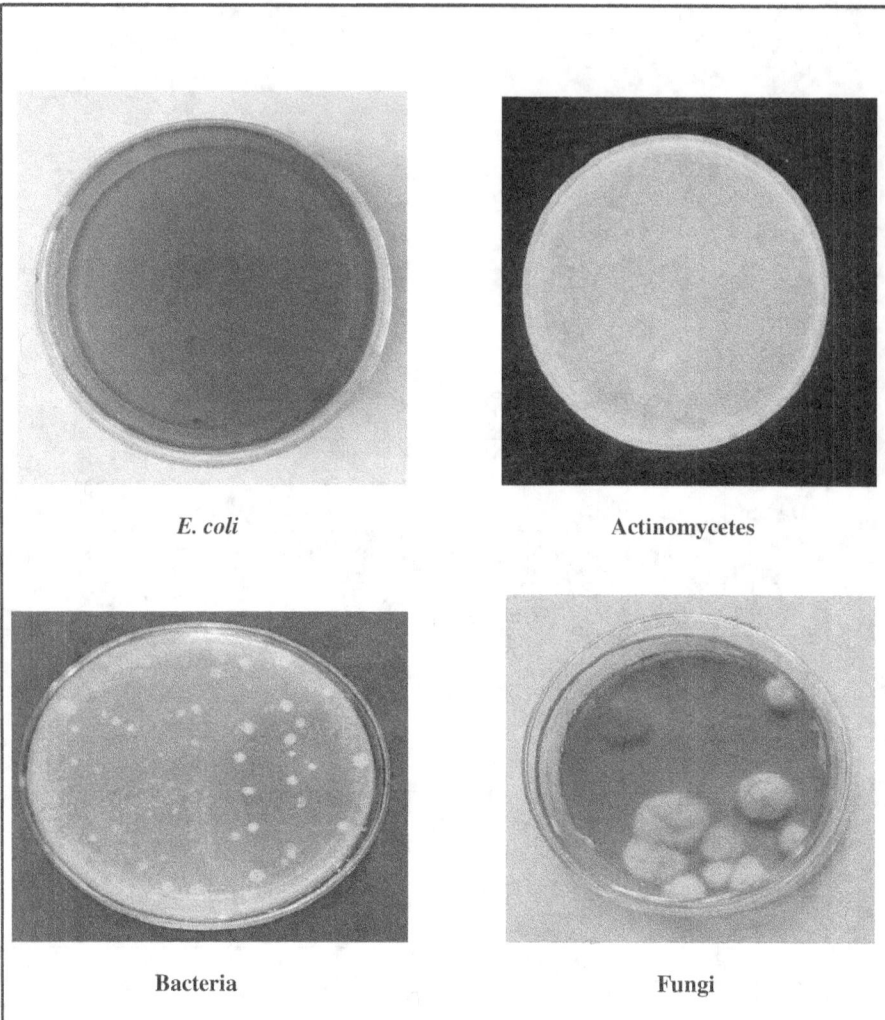

E. coli   Actinomycetes

Bacteria   Fungi

Plate 8. Microbial quality of composite mix during storage

4.9.1 Antidiabetic property of developed composite mix

Antidiabetic property was assessed by *in vitro* method and results are presented in Fig 17. Inhibition of alpha amylase was significantly lower in composite mix (57.00) than in mature jackfruit flour (77.44). However, alpha glucosidase inhibition was recorded to be similar in both composite mix and mature jackfruit flour (64.00 and 64.72% respectively).

4.9.2 Predicted glycemic index of developed composite mix

Utilizing the starch digestibility at 90 min the glycemic index was predicted. A perusal of Fig 18 shows that the glycemic index was predicted to be 48.47 in composite mix and 54.75 in mature jackfruit flour.

4.9.3 Glycemic response of Non-diabetics volunteers

The glucose response of capillary blood, to the consumption of mature jackfruit based composite mix chapathi among non-diabetic subjects was estimated and results are presented in table 33, Fig 19, 20 .

Table 33 shows anthropometric measurements of subjects selected for Glycemic Index. Mean age of the subjects was 34 ±3 years with range from 31 to 39 years. Height of subjects ranged from 152.4 to 179.8 cm with mean of 165.21±2.99 cm. Average weight of the subjects was 58.3±5.33 kg ranging from 49 to 61 kg, Body Mass Index when calculated was 21.29±1.45 ranging 18.55-23.08. Waist Circumference (cm) was 86.66±3.81 (range- 76.2 to 91.44). Average hip circumference of the subjects was 112.39±2.89 cm ranging from 101.6 to 116.84 cm with Waist-Hip Ratio (WHR) of 0.77±0.44.

Fig 19 describes blood glucose response of subjects selected for glycemic index. Mean fasting blood glucose was 91.62 mg/dl when subjects were selected for glucose tolerance test, which increased to 148.87 after 30 min and 161.62 mg/dl aftmer 60 min of feeding. Further, a decline was observed till 120 min to nearly basal level (96.75mg/dl). Five subjects showed blood glucose peak at 60 min and three subjects exhibited peak at 30 min.

On the test meal (chapathi of mature jackfruit based composite mix), fasting blood glucose was 95.25mg/dl which increased to 117.87mg/dl after 30 min of feeding and to 122.50 mg/dl after 60 min. Later a decrease was observed to 93.63mg/dl after 120min.

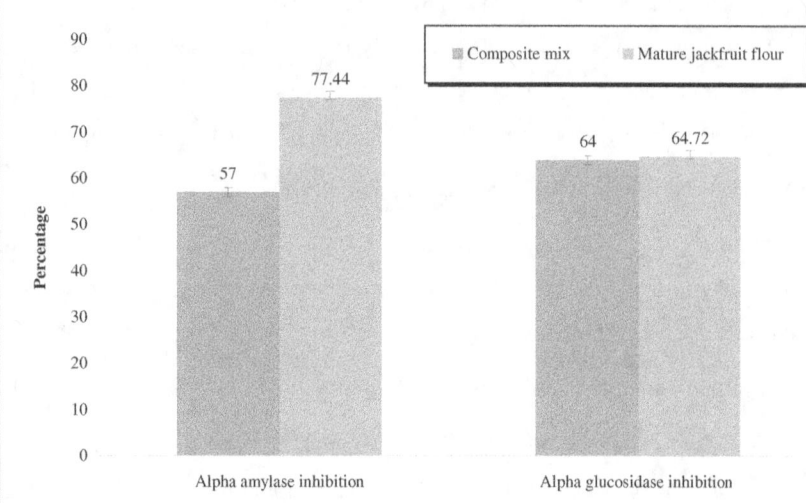

Fig. 17. Antidiabetic property of jackfruit based composite mix

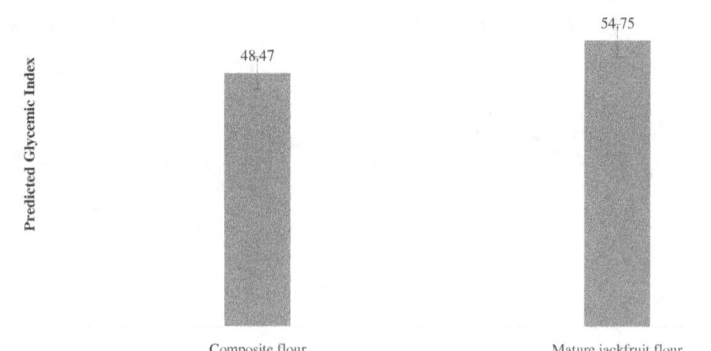

Fig. 18. Predicted glycemic index of composite mix and mature jackfruit flour

Table 33 Anthropometric measurements of subjects selected for Glycemic Index

N-08

Parameters	Mean ±sd	Range
Age (years)	34+2.99	31-39
Height (cm)	165.21±9.7	152.4-179.8
Weight (kg)	58.3±5.33	49-61
Body Mass Index	21.29±1.45	18.55-23.08
Waist Circumference(cm)	86.66±3.81	76.2-91.44
Hip Circumference(cm)	112.39±2.89	101.6-116.84
Waist to Hip Ratio	0.77±0.44	0.67-0.80

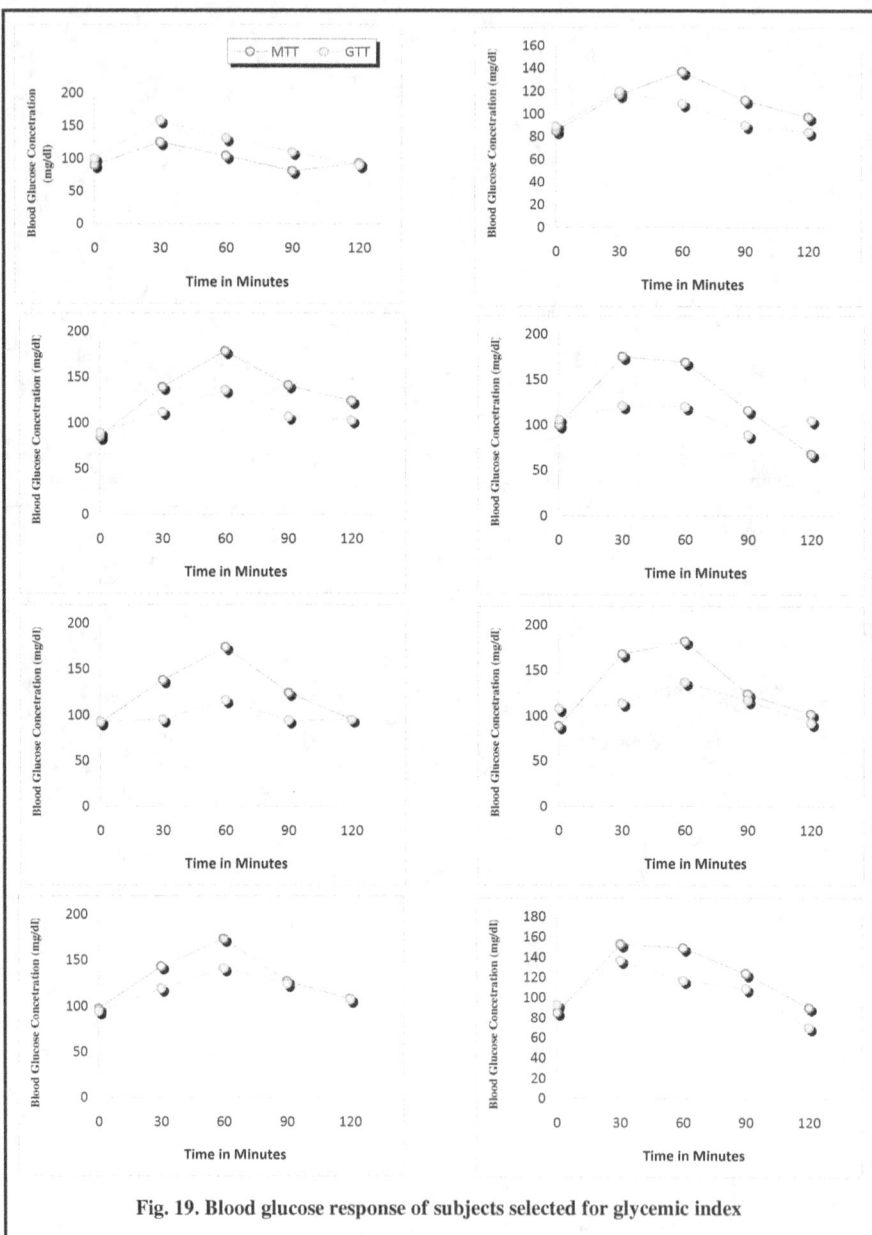

Fig. 19. Blood glucose response of subjects selected for glycemic index

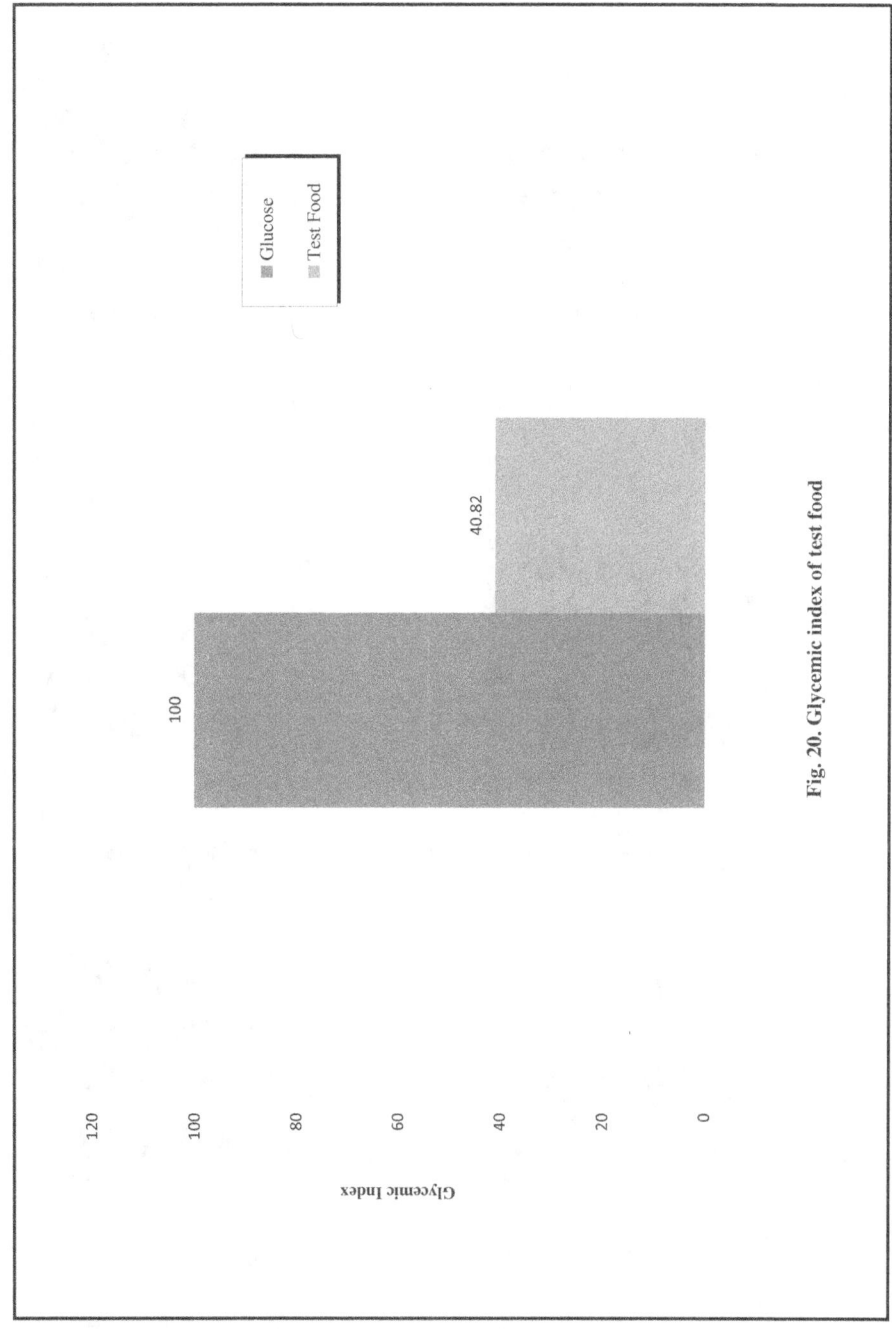

Fig. 20. Glycemic index of test food

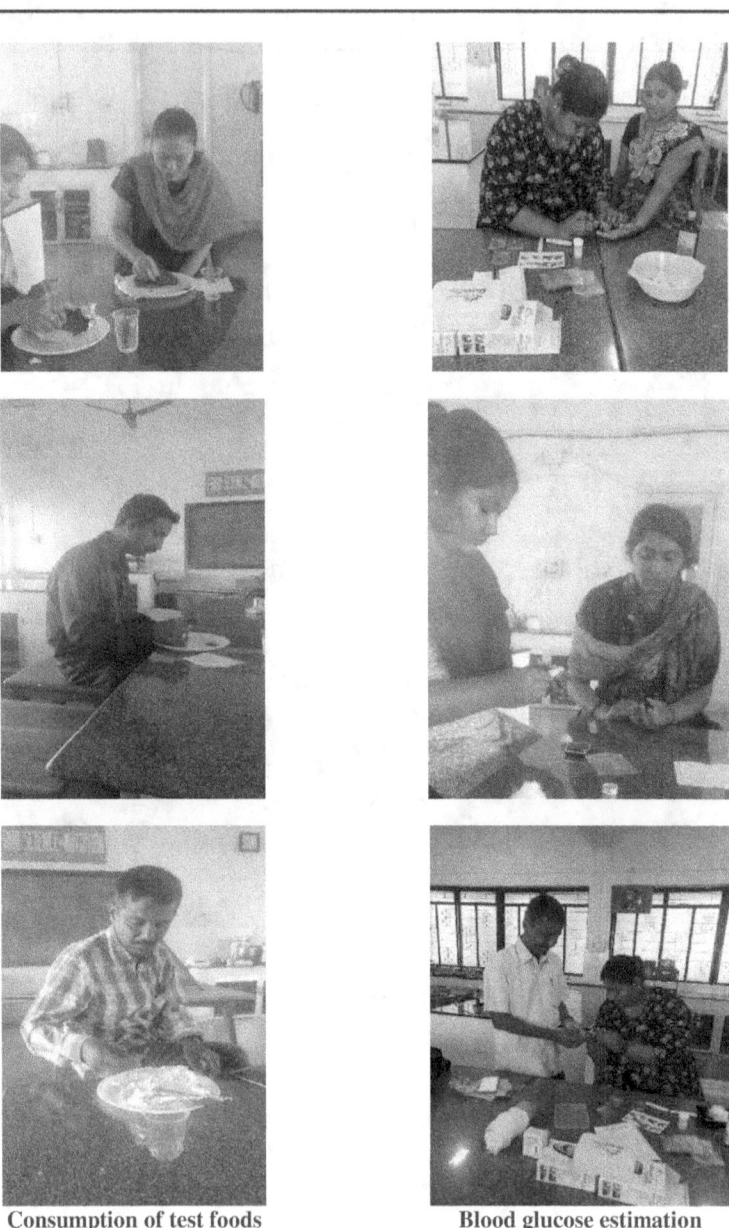

Consumption of test foods   **Blood glucose estimation**

Plate 9. Estimation of in-vivo GI of composite mix

Glycemic index of test food was 40.82 (Fig 20) which fall in low GI category. Glycemic load of developed antidiabetic composite mix is 16.85 which lie under medium glycemic load category.

4.10 ACCEPTABILITY OF DEVELOPED PRODUCT AMONG DIABETIC SUBJECTS

Conducting acceptability among diabetic subjects helps to understand the utility of the products by the target group. Hence, around 31 diabetic patients willing to participate in the study were provided one serving of the product and asked to indicate preference about the product in FACT scale (Plate 10). The results are presented in the following section.

The general information of diabetic subjects selected for acceptability of composite mix is indicated in Table 34. It was observed that out of 31 subjects 62 per cent were males and 38 per cent were females. Mean age of male subjects was 54±6.49 years ranging between 46 to 65 years while that of females was 53±3.95 years ranging between 48 to 63 years. Higher per cent (38.70%) of the subjects were educated upto 10th standard followed by 12th and graduation (29.03%). Very low per cent of subjects (3.22%) were educated upto post-graduation. It was found that 11 out of 12 (35.48%) of the females were housewife, while, 25.80 per cent of the subjects were having government job. Nearly 16 per cent of the subjects were self-employed and farmer each whereas, very low per cent of them (6.45%) were having private job. It was clearly seen from the table that 32.25 each of the subjects were earning less than one lakh rupees and between 1 to 4 lakh rupees annually. Less than 10 per cent of them were earning more than rupees seven lakh. Surprisingly around 55 per cent of the subjects were residing in joint family setup while around 35 and 10 per cent of the subjects were residing in nuclear and extended joint family setups.

Medical history of diabetic subjects selected for acceptability of composite mix is presented in Table 35. It was observed that higher per cent of the subjects (58.06%) were suffering from the disease for more than five years and had at least one another diabetic member in the family while, 42 per cent of them were diagnosed as diabetic for less than five years and did not have any other diabetic person in the family. Nearly 39 per cent of the subjects had diabetic father, 33.33 per cent had diabetic mother and 27.77 per cent of the subjects had diabetic sibling. With respect to exercise pattern it was observed that majority

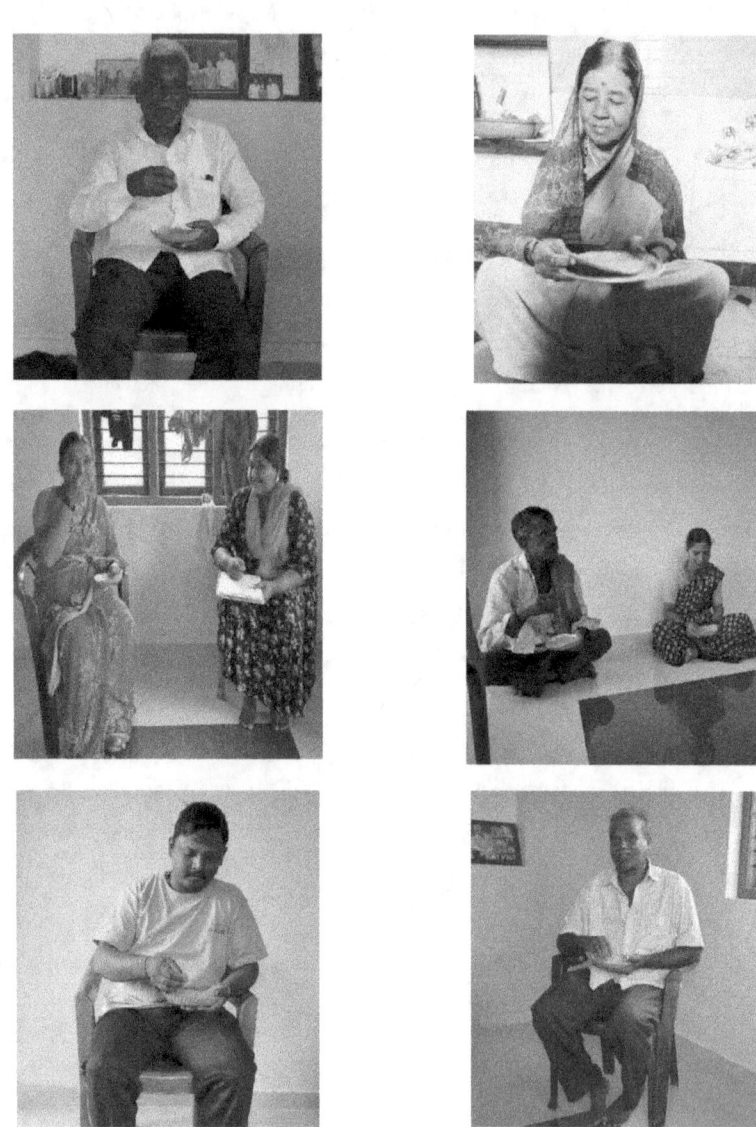

Plate 10. Acceptability of composite mix chapathi by diabetic population

Table 34 General information of diabetic subjects selected for acceptability of composite mix

N-31

Particulars	Details	Number	Percent
Gender			
	Male	19	61.29
	Female	12	38.71
	Total	31	100
Age (years)			
	<50	07	22.58
	51-60	17	54.84
	>60	07	22.58
Education			
	$\leq 10^{th}$	12	38.72
	12th standard	09	29.03
	Graduation	09	29.03
	Post-graduation	01	3.22
Occupation			
	Government Job	08	25.83
	Private job	02	06.45
	Self employed	05	16.12
	House wife	11	35.48
	Farmer	05	16.12
Annual income			
	< one lakh	10	32.25
	1 - 4 lakh	10	32.25
	4.99 - 7 lakh	08	25.83
	More than 7 lakh	03	09.67
Type of family			
	Nuclear	11	35.48
	Joint	17	54.84
	Joint and extended	03	09.68

Table 35 Medical history of diabetic subjects selected for acceptability of composite mix

N-31

Duration of Diabetes			
	Less than five years	13	41.83
	More than five years	18	58.07
Family history of diabetes			
Yes		18	58.06
Relationship with diabetic member			
	Father	07	22.58
	Mother	06	19.35
	Siblings	05	16.12
	No	13	41.95
Exercise pattern$			
	Walking	23	74.19
	Pranayama	17	54.83
	Yoga	12	38.70
Types of medicines consumed			
	Ayurveda	03	9.68
	Allopathy	22	70.96
	On insulin	06	19.36
Medicine$			
	Metformin	21	67.47
	Metformin +Glimepiride	7	22.58
	Metformin + Ayurveda	2	6.45
	Metformin + Avandryl +multivitamins	8	25.80
	Ayurveda	1	3.22
Frequency of insulin		Pattern	
Once a day	1	06 units, (AF) Evening	
Twice a day	4	10 units (BF) Morning+10 Unit (BF) Night	
		10 unit(BF) Morning +18 unit (BF) Night	
		04 Unit(BF) Morning +04 unit (BF) Night	
		06 Unit(BF) Morning +06 unit (BF) Night	
Thrice a day	1	08units (2 units each morning, afternoon and night)	

$ multiple answers possible

(74.19%) of the subjects were practicing walking followed by pranayama (54.83%) and yoga (38.70 %). Majority (70.96%) of the subjects were on allopathic treatment, while less than 10 per cent of the subjects were taking ayurvedic medicine. Six of the subjects (19.35) were on insulin treatment. Higher per cent (67.47%) of the subjects were taking metformin as diabetic medicine followed by 25.80 per cent of them taking metformin along with avandryl and multivitamins. Nearly 23 per cent of the subjects were prescribed to take metformin along with glimepiride, metformin and ayurvedic medicine (6.45%). Only one subject (3.22%) was on ayurvedic medicine. Details of insulin shots indicated that out of six subjects on insulin, four of them were taking twice a day while one subject each were on either once or thrice a day.

The anthropometric measurements of diabetic subjects selected for acceptability of composite mix is presented in Table 36. Mean weight of male subjects was 71.47±9.82 kg and was 59.5±8.26 kg for females. Mean height of male subjects was 172.05±10.22 cm and for females it was 157.90±6.94 cm. Average BMI (kg/m^2) of male and female subjects was 23.85±2.73 and 23.46±2.14 respectively. Majority of the male subjects (63.14%) were having BMI of more than 23 followed by 36.84 per cent of them having between 18.5 and 22.9, but in case of females half of them were having BMI of more than 23 and remaining 50 per cent were having between 18.5 to 22.9. Both diabetic men and women were having WHR of 0.85 and 0.80 respectively, with BAI values of 26.80 and 36.90. Irrespective of gender around 68 per cent were having BAI of more than 35.

The food habits and consumption pattern of diabetic subjects selected for acceptability of composite mix is revealed in Table 37. Higher per cent of subjects (45.16%) were non-vegetarians while 41.93 per cent were vegetarians. With respect to number of meals per day it was seen that 32.26 per cent each of the subjects were having four and six meals a day followed by 19.35 per cent having five meal pattern and only 16.13 per cent of the subjects were consuming more than six meals in a day. With regards to modification of normal diet it was observed that majority (67.75%) of the subject modified their normal diet. Around 48 per cent of the subjects were following diet recommended by dietician whereas, 28.57 and 23.80 per cent of them were practicing recommendations of doctor and self modification respectively.

Table 36 Anthropometric measurements of diabetic subjects selected for acceptability of composite mix

N-31

Particulars	Male	Female	Combined
Age (yrs)	54±6.49	53±3.95	54±5.52
Weight(kg)	71.47±9.82	59.5±8.26	65.48±9.04
Height(cm)	172.05±10.22	157.90±6.94	164.97±8.58
BMI(kg/m2)	23.85 ±2.73	23.46±2.14	23.69±2.52
<18.5	0.00	0.00	0.00
18.5-22.9	7(36.84)	6(50.00)	13(41.94)
>23	12(63.14)	6(50.00)	18(58.06)
Waist circumference (cm)	86.36	79.91	83.14
Hip circumference (cm)	102.66	110.66	106.66
WHR	0.85 ±0.03	0.80±0.03	0.83±0.38
BAI	26.8±4.8	36.9±5.4	30.72±7
>35	3(15.8)	7(58.3)	10(32.26)
<35	16(84.21)	5(42.7)	21(67.74)

Note: BMI: basal metabolic rate, WHR: waist to hip ratio, BAI: body adiposity index

Table 37 Food habit and consumption pattern of diabetic subjects selected for acceptability of composite mix

N=31

Particulars	Number	Percent
Type of food consumption		
Vegetarian	13	41.93
Non vegetarian	14	45.16
Egg based	4	12.90
No. of meals per day		
Four meal pattern	10	32.25
Five meal pattern	6	19.35
Six meal pattern	10	32.25
More than six meals	5	16.14
Modification of normal diet		
Yes	21	67.75
No	10	32.25
Diet recommendation		
Doctor	6	28.57
Dietician	10	47.61
Self	5	23.80

Note: Values in parenthesis indicate percentages

The foods specially added, restricted and avoided by the diabetic subjects selected for acceptability of composite mix are presented in Table 38. Salad, sprouts, little millet, foxtail millet, sorghum, ragi, legumes and pulse, vegetables (except few tubers) were consumed daily by the diabetic subjects. Special supplements like stevia powder (29.03%), Aloe vera juice (25.81%), amla and Noni juice (19.35% each), multigrain atta (16.13%), *methi* seeds and papaya leaf juice (12.90% each) were included in their diet as low glycemic foods. About three per cent of the subjects also included *jamun* seed powder, bitter gourd, *sadabahar* leave juice, wheat grass juice and banana flower to reduce blood glucose level.

While *payasa* (90.32%), rice (83.87%), wheat *chapathi* (48.39%) and jaggery (48.39%) were restricted, white sugar, sweets potatoes, and fried foods were totally avoided by all the subjects.

Table 39 represents the biochemical parameters and co-morbidities of diabetic subjects selected for acceptability of composite mix. Haemoglobin ranged from 10.00 to 14.50 g/dl with mean value of 12.00±1.15 g/dl. The range of fasting and post prandial blood glucose was 110 mg/dl to 307 mg/dl and 154 to 275 mg/dl respectively with mean value of 129±35 mg/dl and 186.00 mg/dl. HBA1C (%) ranged from 6.1 to 10.2. Diastolic blood pressure ranged from 70mmHg to 110 mmHg while, systolic ranged from 110mmHg to 180 mmHg. The mean values for systolic and diastolic blood pressure were 131.45±19mmHg and 83.71±10mmHg respectively. Acidity (25.80%), cataract (22.58%), leg cramps, headache (19.35%) were the other problems experienced by the respondents.

The knowledge of selected subjects regarding diabetes is depicted in Fig 21. Majority (67.74%) of the subjects were having knowledge about diabetes while by 32.25 per cent of them said they do not have knowledge about diabetes. With regard to source of information 40.00 per cent each of the respondents gathered information from electronic media and social media, while only 20.00 per cent of them received information from print media. Nearly 58 per cent of the respondents were aware about availability of designed diabetic foods. Around 39 per cent were interested in purchasing designed diabetic foods only when recommended while equal percent were not interested in purchasing but 22.58 per cent purchased designed diabetic food.

The acceptability of mature jackfruit based composite mix by the diabetic subjects is presented in Table 40. It was observed that maximum number (35.48%) of the respondents

Table 38. Foods included, restricted and avoided by the diabetic subjects selected for acceptability of composite mix

Common foods consumed daily[#]	Low GI food included in diet (%)		Food avoided (%)		Food excluded[#]
Salad	Stevia Powder	29.03	Payasa	90.32	Potato
Sprouts	Aloe Vera Juice	25.81	Rice	83.87	White Sugar
Little Millet	Noni Juice	19.35	Jaggery	48.39	Sweets
Foxtail Millet	Amla Juice	19.35	Wheat chapathi	48.39	Fried foods
Jowar	Multigrain Atta	16.13			
Ragi	Menthe Seeds	12.90			
Legumes and pulses	Papaya Leaf Juice	12.90			
Vegetables (except few tubers)	Nigella Seeds	6.45			
	Banana Flower	3.23			
	Wheat Grass Juice	3.23			
	Jamun Seed Juice	3.23			
	Bitter Gourd	3.23			
	Sadabahar Leaves Juice	3.23			

- all respondents

Table 39 Biochemical parameters and co-morbidities of diabetic subjects selected for acceptability of composite mix

N-31

Parameters	Mean	Minimum	Maximum
Haemoglobin (mg/dl)	12.00±1.15	10	14.5
Fasting blood glucose (mg/dl)	129±35	110	307
Post prandial blood glucose (mg/dl)	186±35	154	275
HBA1C (%)	-	6.1	10.2
Blood pressure (mmHg)			
Systolic	131.45 ±19	110	180
Diastolic	83.71±10	70	110
Other problems experienced by respondents			
Heart (CAD, Arrethymia)	3(9.67)		
Acidity	8(25.80)		
Kidney (CKD,UTI)	2(6.45)		
Eye(cataract)	7(22.58)		
Skin (itching, rashes)	3(9.67)		
Other Problems (leg cramps, headache)	6(19.35)		

Note: Values in parenthesis indicate percentages, CAD: Chronic Artery Diseases, CKD: Chronic Kidney Diseases, UTI: Urinary Tract Infection

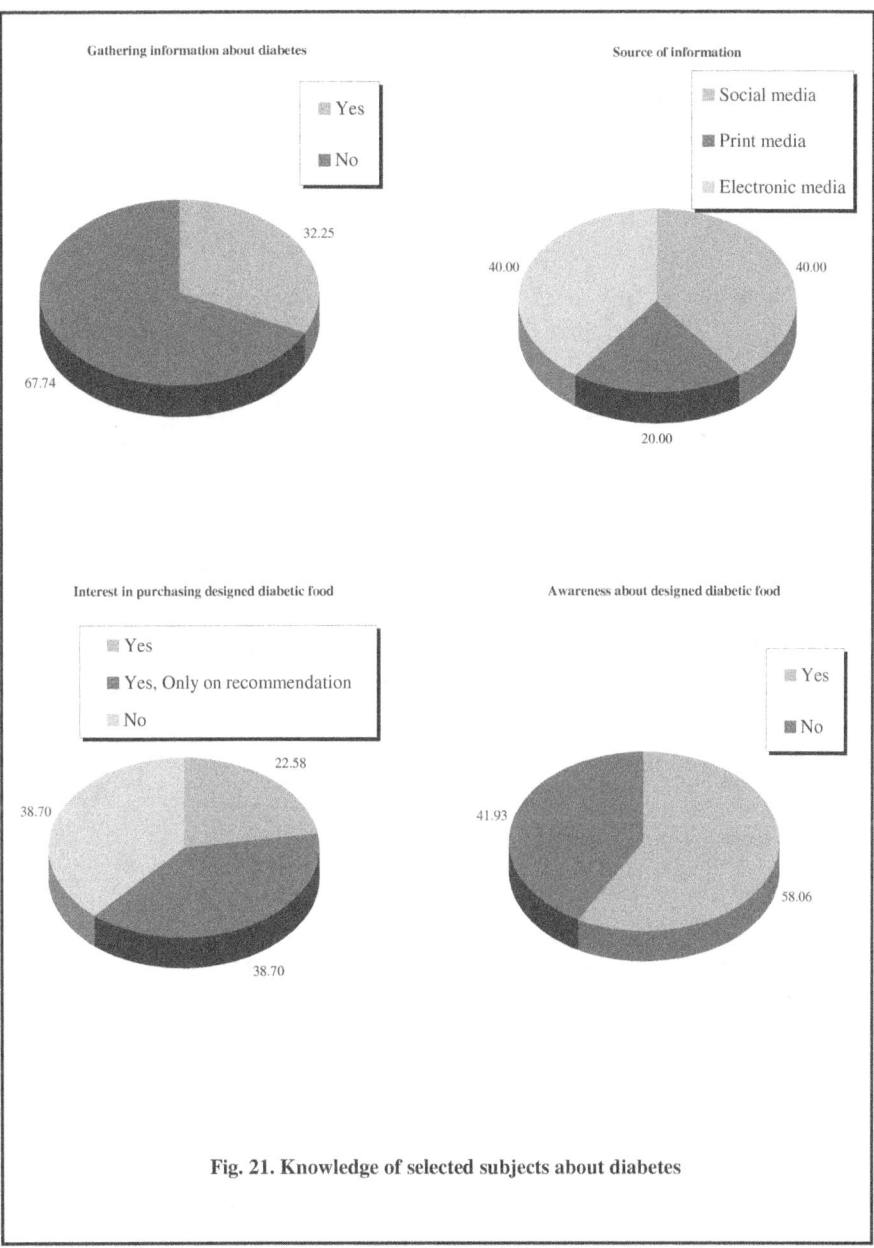

Fig. 21. Knowledge of selected subjects about diabetes

said that they like it and would eat it. Around 13 per cent opined that they eat it often. Twenty five out of 31 (80.65 %) liked the *chapathi* prepared with antidiabetic composite mix while six of them (19.35%) did not like but said they would eat if forced.

4.11 COST OF VALUE ADDED JACKFRUIT BASED PRODUCTS

Table 41 and 42 presents the cost for the preparation of mature jack fruit flour and antidiabetic composite mix. The cost includes variable cost (ingredients cost and labour cost) and fixed cost (building, equipment etc.). Cost per kg of jackfruit flour (Table 41) was Rs. 270 and Rs. 185 respectively when five and 50 kg was prepared. The cost of preparation of mature jackfruit based antidiabetic mix (Table 42) was Rs. 272.00 and Rs. 185 respectively when five and 50 kg were prepared.

Table 40. Acceptability of mature jackfruit based composite mix using FACT scale

Sl. No.	Opinion	Score	Consumer
1.	I would eat this every opportunity that I have	9	3 (9.68)
2.	I would eat this very often	8	4 (12.9)
3.	I would frequently eat this	7	2(6.45)
4.	I like this and would eat it now and then	6	11(35.49)
5.	I would eat if available but would not go out of my way	5	5 (16.13)
6.	I don't like this but would eat this on an occasion	4	0
7.	I would hardly eat this	3	2(6.45)
8.	I would eat this if there were no other food choices	2	0
9.	I would eat this only if forced	1	4 (12.9)

Note: figures in parenthesis indicate percentages
Score: 5.61 (9X3+8X4+7X2+6X11+5X5+3X2+1X4)/31

Table 41. Cost estimation of jack fruit flour

Sl. No.	Particulars	5kg		50kg	
		Quantity (kg)/no.	Total cost In rupees	Quantity (kg)/no.	Total cost In rupees
I	**Variable cost**				
A	*Ingredient cost*				
1	Jackfruit	13	200	130	796
2	Coconut oil	100 ml	36	300	72
3	Packaging material	10	24	100	124
	SUBTOTAL A		**260**		**992**
B	*Labour cost*		350		350
1	Labour cost (1 day)	1	350	1	350
C	**SUBTOTAL B**		**350**		**350**
II	**Fixed cost**				
1	Building rent	-	-	-	3000
2	Rsw103 tray dryer	1	50000	1	50000
3	Weighing balance	1	3000	1	3000
4	Flour milling machine	1	20000	1	20000
5	Small equipments	-	1000	-	3000
	Total		74,000		79,000
	Depreciation	@ 1percent	740	@ 10 percent	7900
	Subtotal (C)		**740**		**7,900**
III	Total cost of production subtitle (A+B+C)		1350		9242

Cost per kg of jackfruit flour was 270.00 and 185.00 when 5 kg or 50 kg was prepared.

Table 42. Cost estimation of jack fruit based antidiabetic composite mix

Sl.No.	Particulars	5KG		50KG	
		Quantity (kg)/no.	Total cost (in Rs.)	Quantity (kg)/no.	Total cost (in Rs.)
I	**Variable cost**				
A	*Ingredient cost*				
1	Jackfruit flour	2.50	462.50	25000	19710
2	Wheat flour	2.50	200.00	25000	2000
3	Dried coriander leaves	3.00	54	3000	540
4	Dried green chilli	0.025	31	250	310
5	Pepper powder	0.025	50	250	500
6	Coriander powder	0.050	30	500	300
7	Packaging material	10	24	100	124
	SUBTOTAL A		**851.50**		**23360**
B	*Labour cost*		350		350
1	Labour cost(1 day)	1	350	1	350
	SUBTOTAL B		**350**		**350**
C	*Fixed Cost*				
	Mixer Grinder	1	5,000	1	5,000
	Weighing balance	1	3,000	1	5,000
	Mixer/Blender	1	5,000	1	5,000
	Ribbon blender	-	-	1	
	Sealing machine	1	2,000	1	2,000
	Minor equipment	1	1,000	1	1000
			16,000		
	Depreciation	@ 1 percent	160.00	@ 10 percent	
	Subtotal (C)		**160.00**		**2500**
III	Total cost of production subtitle (A+B+C)		**1361.50**		**26210.00**

Cost per kg of mature jackfruit based antidiabetic composite mix was 272.00 and 185.00 when 5 kg or 50 kg was prepared.

CHAPTER -5

DISCUSSION

Jackfruit (*Artocarpus heterophyllus*), a tropical fruit being native to Southeast Asia (Boning, 2006) is widely grown and consumed in India. It is underutilized fruit as its usage is restricted to a segment of population. It is also popular as largest tree borne fruit in the world (FAO, 2012). The fruits are consumed in immature, mature and in ripe stage. Major usage is in the form of dessert when ripe and vegetable when unripe. Other uses include fodder, timber, fuel and medicinal and industrial products. Lush green fruit in immature tender form is used in the preparation of vegetables, pickle, chips etc., (Table 3) while, aromatic, pleasant ripe bulbs are used for table purpose and to prepare delicacies like papads, jams, custards, ice creams, other sweets as well as used in daily preparations. The seeds of mature and ripe fruits are used roasted, boiled or fried, (Sreelatha *et al*, 2018) alternately they are mashed or powdered and used in various preparations and medicinal uses. The jackfruit growing farmers of Sirsi opined that animals fed with mesocarp and spiny peel produced higher amounts of milk having high fat content (Personal communication).

Jackfruit is rich in many nutrients specially vitamins and minerals. Though low in carbohydrates, it contains considerable amounts of protein and fiber. Fruit in young and ripe stage contains good amounts of flavonoids, carotenoids and many more phytochemicals. Hence it serves number of roles in protecting human health. Immature and mature fruits possess many health promoting components compared to ripe (Trindade *et al*., 2006; Arora and Parley, 2016). Presence of phytocompounds indicates that jackfruit is used as cancer preventive, antimicrobial, immunoprotective, hypoglycemic agent. Present study was planned to assess the differences between different stages of maturity and to develop antidiabetic composite mix. Further, it was planned to study the nutrient composition, shelf life and antidiabetic property of the developed mix. The results obtained are discussed in the present chapter under different subheads.

5.1 COMPOSITIONAL VARIATION IN DIFFERENT STAGES OF MATURITY OF JACKFRUIT

Physical properties including morphological parameters play a significant role in acceptance, marketability and utility by the consumers. The weight, diameter, both lengthwise and widthwise circumferences and other physical properties change with maturation and ripening (Shamsudin *et al*, 2009). In the present study, length, breadth, lengthwise circumference and weight of inedible portion increased markedly from immature stage to mature and ripe stage (Table 5) whereas, widthwise circumference decreased. This indicates that fruit grows lengthwise resulting in changes in shape. Increase in peel thickness, rags, perianth and other parts leads to increase in inedible portion. However, not much variation between mature and ripe fruits was observed which indicates that variations are detectable in internal composition rather than size, and external morphological growth was completed by mature stage. The results of the present study are in accordance with that of many scientists (Haq, 2006; Sidhu, 2012; and Rana *et al.*, 2018)

Proximate composition including macro and micro nutrients plays an important role in deciding the nutritional benefit of the food. Macro nutrients like carbohydrates, protein and fat perform basic functions, while, micro nutrients – vitamins and minerals support the macro nutrients. The moisture content decreased with maturity and increased again during ripening. Similar results were observed by Ong *et al.* (2006); Ranasinghe and Marapana, (2019). In the present study, protein, ash, carbohydrate and energy contents of mature fruits were higher than other two stages (Table 6), while the moisture and crude fiber contents were lower. On the contrary, mineral content decreased with increase in maturity and ripening (Table 7), probable due to utilization of minerals during growth.

Total starch, amylopectin and resistant starch increased from immature stage to mature stage and decreased with ripening (Table 8). Initial increase from immature to mature can be reasoned to deposition of starch globules on maturity and further decrease could be due to the conversion of starch to sugars and other soluble carbohydrates (Selvraj and Pal, 1989; Goswami *et al.*, 2011; and Shamla *et al.*, 2019). However, lower values of total starch (2.23%) were reported by Jagadeesh *et al.*, (2007); Goswami *et al.*, (2011); and Tiwari and Vidyarthi (2015). As stated by Jagadeesh and coworkers (2007), varieties of jackfruit vary in their capacity to accumulate starch and also amylase activity varies from one variety to another, which certainly results in changes in rates of hydrolyses of starch of genetically dissimilar selections. Further, the variations in climatic conditions and growing situations cannot be ruled out. The total sugar content increased tremendously from immature stage to ripe stage owing to hydrolysis of starch to sugars as there was a concurrent decrease in starch in ripe stage. Similar results of increase in total sugar content on ripening have been reported by several scientists (Jagadeesh *et al.*, 2007; Tiwari and Vidyarthi 2015; Ong *et al.*, (2006);

Goswami *et al.*, 2011). Significant increase in dietary fiber content observed in the present study confirms the observation of Rahman *et al.*, (1999) who reported an increase in carbohydrate and dietary fiber with maturity. On ripening there was a slight decrease in dietary fiber content probably due to solubilisation and breakdown of pectin to its individual fragments like galacturonic acid (Brecht and Ritenour, 2018 PPT).

5.2 NUTRITIONAL QUALITY OF JACKFRUIT AT DIFFERENT STAGES OF MATURITY

In vitro digestibilities reflect the utilizabilities of nutrients. The *in vitro* studies are equally effective in depicting the availability of nutrients to the body and are time saving and do not require invasion in the human body. One of the macronutrient is protein, which is responsible for human growth and development. All proteins are not digested totally in the human body; protein digestibility indicates susceptibility of protein to hydrolysis. Higher the digestibility better is the amino acid profile and higher the quality of that protein.

As stated by Pushparaj and Urooj (2011) digestibility of proteins is influenced by many exogenous factors *viz.*, interaction of proteins with non-protein components like starch, lipids, polyphenols, tannins, phytates, dietary fibre, non-starch polysaccharides, and endogenous factors *viz.*, changes within the proteins themselves. Several antinutritional factors such as enzyme inhibitors, phytates, lectins, tannins *etc.* are known to interfere with mineral bioavailability, carbohydrate and protein digestibility (Malik 2002, Sehgal and Kwatra 2006 and Sade 2009). In the present study, the *in vitro* protein digestibility was lower in immature jackfruit while not much difference was noticed in mature and ripe fruits (Fig 5). This may be due to the presence of inhibiting factors like phenols (Fig 7) and absence of few essential amino acids (Shamla *et al.*, 2019).

Starch is an important constituent of total carbohydrates and plays significant functional role in food processing besides providing energy to the human body. Different components of starch like amylose, amylopectin, resistant starch are of importance in the present era of escalating non communicable diseases like diabetes, cardio-vascular diseases, cancer, obesity *etc.* Higher the resistant starch, lower is the digestibility and raise in blood sugar. Such foods are essential while planning low glycemic meal. The results of current study indicated that immature jackfruit having low starch digestibility (Table 9), contained lower amounts of rapid and slow digestible starch. Surprisingly ripe jackfruit contained higher amounts of slow digesting starch while in mature fruit there was no difference in slow and rapid digesting starch. Presence of slow digesting starch indicates probably the occurrence of non-starch polysaccharides like pectins, fibers etc.

The starch which gets digested slowly in the small intestine and releases glucose at reduced pace into the blood stream is known as slow digestible starch. Slowly digestible starch (SDS) leads to low glycemic response (Englyst and others 1992; Bj örck and others 2000; Ells and others 2005; Aston2006). The SDS is beneficial in lowering the glycemic index, and thus, is related to reduction of the risk of diverse chronic degenerative diseases such as type 2 diabetes, overweight and obesity (Jenkins and others 2002; Brand-Miller *et al.,* 2007).

5.3 ANTIOXIDANT COMPONENTS AND ACTIVITY OF JACKFRUIT AT DIFFERENT STAGES OF MATURITY

Antioxidants are substances that scavenge free radicals produced due to either stress, faulty food habits, pollution etc. Though BHA and BHT are synthetic antioxidants (Gomathi *et al.,* 2014, Siddiqi, 2015). Many natural antioxidants are available in food like polyphenols, dietary fiber, flavonoids, carotenoids and alike that are most often non-nutritive substances. These components also play the role of providing protection to plants as secondary metabolites. Many scientific research suggested the role of polyphenols, anthocyanins, carotenoids and flavonoids present in fruits, vegetables, spices and other foods as natural antioxidants and these components help to scavenge free radicals and thus protects cellular damage (Benvenuti, Pellati, Melegari, & Bertelli, 2004; Pietta, 2000). Phenolic compounds are also very important plant constituents because their hydroxyl groups confer the scavenging ability and considerable *in vitro* antioxidant and antidiabetic activity (Cares *et al.* 2009). In the present study, the amount of phenols was higher in immature and ripe fruits while tannins were higher in mature and ripe fruits. Astringency and high amounts of browning seen in immature fruit (Fig.7) is indicator of presence of phenols. This presence of higher amounts of antioxidant components in immature fruit has translated into higher antidiabetic property in terms of inhibition of alpha glucosidase and alpha amylase (Fig 8).

The antioxidants act either by scavenging the reactive oxygen species or protecting the antioxidant defense mechanism (Halliwell *et al,* 2004). Metal chelating capacity is significant since it reduces the concentration of the transition metal that catalyzes lipid peroxidation. The electron donation ability of natural products can be measured by using methanol solution of 2,2'-diphenyl-1- picrylhydrazyl radical (DPPH). DPPH is a very stable free radical. In the present study immature fruits possessed significantly higher capacity to neutralize DPPH compared to other two stages (Table 10). Nair (2013) also reported significantly greater capacity of jackfruit to neutralize DPPH.

5.4 ANTIDIABETIC PROPERTY OF JACKFRUIT AT DIFFERENT STAGES OF MATURITY

Glycemic index (GI) is the measure of immediate effect on blood glucose level after food consumption whereas starch digestibility index is relative rate of starch digestion (Odenigbo et al. 2012). Starch digestibility has been associated with the glycemic index (GI) and it helps to assess the therapeutic quality of foods. The GI indicates postprandial glucose response of starchy foods, which are characterized and classified based on glucose response (Jenkins and others 1981; Miao and others 2015).

In the present study, immature jackfruit was predicted to have lower glycemic index followed by mature and ripe (Fig 9). Besides phenolic compounds, starch properties, starch components, presence of resistant starch, amylopectin, dietary fiber and many more such components determine the glycemic index. Glycemic load reflects both quantity and quality of carbohydrate while glycemic index takes into account only the quality of carbohydrate. The, glycemic load of immature and ripe jackfruits in the present study, were lower than mature owing to the amount of carbohydrate present per serving. In the present study, though there was variation in glycemic load, fruits of all three stages could be grouped under low glycemic load as per Brand et al., (1991) and Miller et al., (1992). Compared to amylopectin, amylose undergoes staling readily after cooking as it has a linear structure. The resultant resistant starch is then metabolized similarly to dietary fibre in the large intestine or colon. Thus effect of cooking also affects lowering of GI (Panlasigui et al. 1991).

5.5 VALUE ADDITION TO JACKFRUIT OF DIFFERENT STAGES OF MATURITY

Fruits and vegetables are perishable foods with life of a few days or weeks under ambient conditions which extends to a few weeks under refrigeration. They are the treasure trove of nutrients especially micronutrients and thus, help to mitigate hidden hunger, the most prevalent problem in India. On one side the per capita consumption of fruits and vegetables fails to meet ICMR recommendation, on the other, huge proportion of fruits and vegetables get wasted (16%) for want of proper storage conditions, processing technologies, distance to be travelled from farm to processing plant and many more (Sharma *et al.*, 2019). Under such circumstances processing for value addition is the need of the hour to avoid wastage and to preserve this group of foods to provide micronutrient security. According to Sharma and associates (2014), the process of increasing economic value and consumer appeal of an agricultural commodity by transforming its original form through various techniques like processing, preservation, freezing, simple grading, packing and labeling is called value addition. Traditional methods of preservation include pickling and drying. Drying has the advantage of reduction in weight, concentration of nutrients, ease of transportation, and facilitates incorporation in many traditional preparations. Added advantage is hindrance of growth of microorganisms owing to reduced water activity (Doymaz and Pala, 2003).

Though jackfruit has tough peel with spikes, it has shelf life of 180-210 days. According to Satheeshan and coworkers (2019), jackfruit has a great potential for value addition to minimize post-harvest losses and to enhance non-seasonal availability of the fruit. With progression of process of ripening many physical, chemical, sensorial and microbial changes are bound to happen along with changes in health promoting factors. In the present study, jackfruit in different stages of maturity was dehydrated to get flour as a value added product. Flour was further investigated for quality and an attempt was made to fabricate a composite mix suitable for diabetic population.

Immature and mature jackfruit could be dehydrated within 6-8 hrs and powdered to get flour. However, owing to high sugar content, ripe stage could not be dehydrated to crispness and could not be powdered. The powder obtained with difficulty exhibited high level of hygroscopicity, hence could not be further researched. Since moisture content of immature and mature fruits was in the range of 75 to 80 per cent (Table 6) flour yield was 20 and 26 per cent in immature and mature fruits (Table 14).

Balamaze *et al.*, (2019) reported dry matter content of 22 to 26 per cent in jackfruits of different varieties. This justifies the flour yield in the present study (Table 14). Mature fruits having considerably completely developed bulbs, perianth, rags might have had lower moisture and thus, higher flour yield. Immature fruit flour was acidic while mature was towards neutrality (Table 14). Similar near neutral pH of 6.08 to 6.21 in jackfruit was reported by Rana *et al.* (2018). Mature flour was more bulkier than immature probably due to more compact arrangement of starch granules. Around one third of both immature and mature flour could pass through 85 mesh sieve and were having particle size of 180microns (Table 15).

Colour is the visual parameter that determines acceptance and is indicator of maturity. With progression of maturity, colour changes in outer morphology and inner fruit are inevitable. As the fruit colour changes, the flour prepared with fruit also changes in colour. The color value L* indicate the lightness from black (0) to white (100), a* indicate green (-) to red (+) and b* indicate blue (-) to yellow (+). The colour of jackfruit flour at different stages of maturity was compared with wheat flour since wheat is common staple flour used in India. Wheat flour was lighter, more towards white, less of redness and yellowness compared to immature, mature and ripe fruit flours (Table 16). Among jackfruit flours, mature jackfruit flour had colour values closer to wheat flour though not same as wheat flour. Immature fruit flour was dark in colour more towards black, followed by ripe. The darkness of immature flour can be reasoned to the presence of higher amounts of polyphenols (Fig 7), and the enzymatic browning (Miller, 1998), while that in ripe fruits can be reasoned to caremalization of high sugar (Table 8) during drying and also the polyphenols and tannins. Enzymatic browning occurs due to the action of polyphenol oxidases when the cut portion gets exposed to oxygen. The reaction of phenolic substrates results in formation of melanin (Miller 1998). The enzymes catalyze the oxidation of phenolic compounds and produce quinones which further undergo polymerization and lead to dark insoluble melanins. (marshall and wei 2000). Presence of higher amounts of total sugar and sugar components lead to non-enzymatic browning i.e. carmalization and thus the color was darker. Drying of fruits results in both enzymatic and non-enzymatic browning (NEB). NEB is the result of development of melanoidins. The colored compunds (Saxena et al., 2012) the reaction between essential amino acids and reducing sugar present in the ripe fruits leads to the formation of colored compounds (Fennemma , 1996).

Besides physical, chemical, phytochemical components, functional properties play a major role in utilization of the flour. As the name indicates functional properties help in functionality of flours in end uses. Functional properties or characteristics reflect the complex interaction between the composition, structure, confirmation and physico-chemical properties of food components and the nature of environment in which these are associated and measured (Kinsella, 1976). Functional characteristics are required to evaluate and possibly help to predict how new proteins, fat, fibre and carbohydrates may behave in specific systems as well as demonstrate whether or not such protein can be used to stimulate or replace conventional protein (Mattil, 1971). Many of the functional properties like water absorption capacity, oil absorption capacity, solubility and swelling power determine the behavior of components of food in a food system and suitability in food preparation. In the present study mature jackfruit flour possessed higher water absorption capacity, oil absorption capacity, swelling power and solubility compared to immature fruit flour. These differences can be attributed to the molecular structure of flours, amount of protein present, the interaction of protein with water and conformational characteristics, particle size of starch granules, presence of hydrophyllic groups, presence of other components like fiber, other polysaccharides, damage to the starch (Kaushal *et al.*, 2012).

It is possible that protein interacts with water present in foods due to the fact that it contains both hydrophyllic and hydrophobic groups. Kuntz and Brassfield (1971) reported that lower water absorption capacity in some flours may be due to less availability of polar amino acids in flours. The increase in water absorption capacity may be due to increase in solubility and loss of starch crystalline structure. The mature fruit flour in the present study (Table 17) with high water absorption may have more hydrophilic constituents such as polysaccharides. The results of current study were in comparison with those reported by Narayana and Rao (1982) in raw and heat processed winged bean flour; Oluwatooyin *et al.* (2003) on parboiling of red and white sweet potato; Odoemelon (2005) on heat processing of jackfruit seed flour; Ejiofor *et al.* (2014) in processed jackfruit seed flour and Akubor and Obiegbuna (2014) in African breadfruit kernel flour on toasting, fermentation and boiling. Higher water absorption suggests its utility in products requiring high viscosity.

Number of intrinsic factors like amino acid composition, protein conformation and surface polarity or hydrophobicity influences the oil absorption capacity of food protein. As protein is composed of both hydrophilic and hydrophobic parts, it is thus a major chemical component affecting oil absorption capacity. Non-polar amino acid side chains can form hydrophobic interaction with hydrocarbon chains of lipids (Jitngarmkusol *et al.* 2008). Variation in non polar side chains of the amino acids on the surface of the protein molecules, which might bind the hydrocarbon side chains of oil in the flours (Adebowale and Lowal, 2004), are responsible for variations in oil absorption capacity. Hence, increased oil absorption capacity of mature fruit flour may be attributed to denaturation and dissociation of constituent proteins (Narayana and Rao, 1982). The results were in comparison with Odoemelon (2005) in raw and heat processed jackfruit seed flour, Abraham and Jayamuthunagai (2014) in raw jackfruit seed flour and Akubor and Obiegbuna (2014) in raw, toasted and boiled African breadfruit kernel flour. The variation may also be due to variation in protein content.

Mature fruit flour possessed higher solubility and swelling power compared to immature fruit flour. Higher amylopectin (Table 8) is responsible for higher swelling power. The extent of swelling depends on the temperature, availability of water, species of starch and other carbohydrates and proteins. The higher amylopectin is primarily responsible for higher granule swelling. Murthy and Ramanujam (1986) reported that the swelling power of granules is an indication of the extent of associative forces within granule. Formation of protein-amylose complex in native starches and flours may be the cause of decrease in swelling power.

Jackfruit in immature, mature and ripe stage was converted to flour which was characterized. The brown colour and astringency of immature fruit flour can be reasoned to higher phenols (Fig 7) and that of ripe flour can be due to caremalization of free sugars produced by hydrolysis of starch to sugars and other soluble carbohydrates. With progress of maturity the deposition of starch globules cannot be ruled out and further progress towards ripening leads to conversion of starch to sugars (Selvraj and Pal, 1989 and Goswami et al., 2011, Shamla et al., 2019). Similar results of browning with time were observed by Mota et al. (1999) in banana flour.

5.6 PHYSICAL AND NUTRITIONAL QUALITY OF ANTIDIABETIC COMPOSITE MIX

Jackfruit is used in the preparation of fresh products like sambhar, dosa, idli, kadabu or incorporation in rice based products (Table 3). Mature jackfruit is used for pickling, papad making or chips preparation. Though these products are highly accepted, they are consumed as adjuncts or in smaller quantity. Further, these foods are not consumed on daily basis. In order to extend intake, it is essential to prepare staple foods that can be consumed regularly and can reap health benefits. Compatible mixture of different flours to enhance nutritive value, health benefits or sensory properties is called composite flour. Generally wheat flour is used as a base since it is a staple for large segment of Indian population and can be used in innumerable preparations. In the present study, jackfruit flour was incorporated into wheat flour to develop composite mix that can be consumed daily as chapathi and consumer can reap the health benefits. Since mature fruit flour had desirable characteristics like white colour, roasted aroma, slight astringency and smooth free flowing texture (Table 18), when converted to composite mix it was accepted at higher proportion in wheat flour as against immature fruit flour. Immature flour turned to be bitter probably due to phenols and other browning compounds like melanoidins. Jackfruit flour had 30 to 40 per cent starch (Table 8) and was devoid of gluten hence, could not possess elasticity. In order to improve elasticity and rolling property into chapathi, trials were undertaken to mix jackfruit flour with wheat flour. Mature fruit flour could be replaced up to 50 per cent in composite mix. Though 50 per cent replacement was accepted, to improve further, spices like coriander leaves, green chilies, pepper powder, coriander seed powder were added (Table 20) and the chapathi was accepted with acceptability index of 82.67 as against 88.62 in wheat chapathi (Fig 10). Advantage of jackfruit flour incorporated chapathi is the keeping quality. The chapathi was soft even after 36 hrs (Table 21). This may be due to high water absorption capacity which was responsible for providing humectancy and moistness. The product was scored between 'like moderately' to 'like very much' for all sensory parameters (Table 22). Acceptability of mature jackfruit based composite mix chapathi was evaluated by the target population i.e. diabetic population. The selected subjects (20 out of 31) liked the product and would eat it often (Table 40). Similar results were found in study conducted by Kadam *et al.*, (2012) Cheng & Bhat (2015) and Menon *et al.*, (2015).

Lightness (L), redness (a), yellowness (b), chroma (c) and hue (h) were estimated for composite mix and chapathi in comparison to wheat flour and wheat chapathi. In the present study composite flour was recorded to be darker than wheat flour and lighter than mature jackfruit flour (Table 23). Redness and yellowness of composite flour were nearer to wheat and lesser than mature fruit flour. The addition of wheat flour might have resulted in dilution of colour thus bringing it closer to wheat flour, but not on par with it. This darkness in color of composite flour may be due to the presence of phenols and other flavanoids. The possibility of enzymatic browning cannot be ruled out in dark colour of composite flour. instrumental measurements of color of jackfruit based composite mix obtained with colorimetry (in CIE and CIE L*a*b* systems) were in good agreement with sensory evaluations of color and appearance, so that composite mix enable to maintain the lowest color changes during storage, that almost cannot be noticed visually, if evaluations are not performed by very experienced and trained panellists. Similar results were depicted in study of Popov and Petronijević (2009).

Particle size of the flours is important for quality attributes like water and oil holding capacity, wettability, dispersion, bulk density etc. Savlak *et al*, (2016) stated that particle size of unripe banana flour affected the viscosity of batter and texture of end product. This makes it important to study particle size of flours. In the present study around 40 per cent particles of composite mix were of 180 microns. Similarly approximately 30 per cent of wheat and mature jackfruit flour were of 180 microns, while very low per cent of fine flour was observed in all three flours.

Foods play many non-nutritive roles besides providing benefits of nutritional security due to the presence of number of non-nutritive substances. These interact with other molecular constituents physically and chemically thus affect the overall behavior in food systems. These non-nutritive substances, called functional ingredients are important in processing, organoleptic parameters, storage and overall quality of foods. Water and oil absorption, solubility, swelling power, pasting, gelation etc. are included as functional properties (Fennema and Tannenbanum, 1996). Water absorption capacity of the developed composite mix was higher than wheat flour and lower than mature jackfruit flour. This can be attributed to higher fiber content of composite mix compared to wheat flour. Eltayeb *et al.*, (2011) in Bambara groundnuts flour (281.35%), Padilla *et al.*, (1996) in soybean flour (130%) and sunflower meal products. Oshadi *et al.*, (1997) in African yam bean flour (118 to 179%) and Adeyeye and Aye, (2005) in lima bean flours (130 to 140%) observed lower value of water absorption capacity. The differences in genetic makeup of the grains might be responsible for such variations. Aziz *et al.* (2011) also reported higher water absorption capacity in green and ripe mango flour compared to wheat flour.

The composite mix contained higher amounts of protein with reduced amounts of energy, fat, crude fiber, total minerals and carbohydrates compared to mature jackfruit flour (Table 26). This can be attributed to higher protein of wheat flour. Further the protein had better digestibility of 88 per cent. As the protein and carbohydrate contents increased the energy which depends on these macronutrients will also increase. The energy content of composite mix and mature jackfruit flour was similar to that of cereals and other grains. When moisture free, the nutrients get concentrated quantitatively, though qualitative changes are inevitable. Reduction of fat and fiber on conversion of mature jackfruit flour into composite mix can be reasoned to lower values in wheat flour as half of the mix is composed of wheat flour. But the values were higher than wheat flour indicating that composite mix serves as better source for providing nutrition security. It has been stated by Baliga *et al.* (2011) that jackfruit contains quantitatively higher nutrients specially protein, minerals and thiamine, compared to other tropical fruits like orange, mango, pineapple, banana, papaya and ber (Bhatia, et al., 1955; Haq, 2006; Kumar,1988).

5.7 ANTIOXIDANT COMPONENTS AND ACTIVITY OF COMPOSITE MIX

Scientists across the globe have reported the presence of many phytochemicals in jackfruit, the concentration of which changes with variety and place of cultivation. (Arung et al., 2007; Chandrika, et al., 2004; Lu & Lin, 1993; Ong *et al.*, 2006; Venkataraman, 2001; Wong, et al., 1992). In the recent years lot of research has been concentrated on polyphenols of fruits, seeds, vegetables, plant extracts etc., after understanding the role of these compounds in preventing various life style disorders such as diabetes, cancer, cardiovascular diseases and alike. Polyphenols are secondary metabolites that offer protection to plants besides functioning as scavengers of free radicals generated in the body. As stated by Cao and Cao, (1999) bioactive compounds found in the fruits, among other plants and herbs have been shown to have possible health benefits with antioxidative, anticarcinogenic, antiatherosclerotic, antimutagenic, and angiogenesis inhibitory activities. Interestingly, many herbs, fruits, and vegetables are known to contain large amounts of phenolic antioxidants other than the well known vitamins C, E, and carotenoids. Phenolic compounds have the capacities to quench lipid peroxidation, prevent DNA oxidative damage, scavenge free radicals (Cao and Cao, 1999 and Peramunagama *et al.*, 2018) and prevent inhibition of cell communication (Sigler and Ruch, 1993), all of which are proven precursors to degenerative diseases. Resveratrol (trans-3,5,4-trihydroxystilbene, RES) is one of the polyphenols naturally present in jackfruit and is well-known for its health-promoting activities of antioxidant, cardio protect, and anti-inflammatory. In the study of Peramunagama *et al.*, (2018) highest total phenolic content was observed in mature stage crude extract (434.04 ± 7.38 mg GAE/g) while lowest value 52.08 ± 7.03 mg GAE/g was reported for ripe stage crude extract. A decline in total phenolic content with progress of maturity and ripening was observed in jackfruit extract. The decline in total phenolic content and total flavonoid content as the fruit reaches its maturity was also observed in the Pawpaw fruit (Harris *et al.* 2009). In the present study composite mix contained higher amounts of phenols and tannins than mature jackfruit flour (Table 28). This can be reasoned to the presence of spices like coriander leaves, pepper, coriander seed powder etc. (Table 20). The values in the present study are much lower than those reported by Peramunagama *et al.*, (2018). This probably was because in the present study composite flour and mature fruit powder were used as against ethanolic extracts used in the study of Peramunagama *et al.*, (2018).

Cereal fibers find a significant place as neutraceuticals in treatment or management of several disorders. However, fruit and vegetable fibers being rich in soluble and total fibers cannot be neglected. These fibers possess higher water and oil holding capacities, colonic fermentability and lower caloric value. Hence are considered of good quality. Soluble fibers constitute pectins, mucillages, gums etc. The combination of cereal flour with fruit flour offers added advantages of both.

Innumerable free radicals will be generated in the human body due to faulty food habits, wrong life style, stress etc. These radicals pose a threat to dispersion of non-communicable diseases like diabetes, cardio-vascular diseases, cancer and many more. To scavenge these free radicals from the body antioxidant have a greater role. Antioxidants are absolutely critical for maintaining optimal cellular and systemic health and well being. Antioxidant based drugs and formulations for the prevention and treatment of complex diseases like Alzheimer's disease and cancer have appeared during last three decades. The antioxidant activity can be assessed by different methods like DPPH, FRAP, ABTS, phosphomolybdenum assay. Prieto *et al.* (1999) states that hydrogen and electron transfer from antioxidant source to DPPH, ABTS and Mo (VI) occurs in DPPH, ABTS and Phosphomolybdenum assay methods. The transfer depends on the structure of antioxidant. DPPH and ABTS methods detect flavonoids and polyphenols while, phosphomolybdenum assay detects antioxidants like ascorbic acid, certain phenolics, vitamin E, and carotenoids. In the present study, DPPH and Molybdenum assays were employed to assess antioxidant activity and capacity of composite mix, DPPH is a stable radical widely used to assess antioxidant activity. The phosphomolybdenum method includes reduction of Mo (VI) to Mo (V) by the developed composite mix. Higher amounts of phenols, tannins and dietary fiber present in the composite mix might have resulted in higher antioxidant activity of mature jackfruit based composite flour (Table 28). Nair (2013) reported a close correlation between the antioxidant capacity and the amount of phenolics, flavonoids, and flavonols present in the plant. Cares *et al.*, (2009) stated that total polyphenols play a vital role in anti oxidization as well as in the biological functions of the plant.

In the present study, the composite flour based on mature jackfruit flour possessed 96 per cent DPPH scavenging activity and 79 per cent phosphomolybdenum reduction. Higher capacity compared to mature jackfruit flour can be reasoned not only to the phenols, dietary fiber and other antioxidant components of jackfruit, but also to the presence of carotenoids, flavonoids and other compounds of wheat flour and spices added to the mix. Similar radical scavenging capacity is reported by Ong *et al.,* (2006), Jagtap, *et al.,* (2010) and Almeida. *et al.*, (2011).

5.8 EFFECT OF STORAGE OF COMPOSITE MIX ON QUALITY

Estimating shelf-life of the any food product is as important as its acceptability within the population. Shelf life is an indicator of keeping quality of the product under specific conditions which is pointer towards entrepreneurship. The quality of the product on storage depends on the combination of ingredients used, packaging material employed, conditions of storage and of course interaction of the ingredients within themselves and with packaging material. Composite mix is blend of multiple ingredients which may have different shelf life solely. Blend can develop better shelf life or may start degrading early. Keeping these in mind storage quality of composite mix was planned and executed for period of six months.

In the present study, high density polyethylene pouches (HDPE) and aluminum coated polyethylene pouches (ALPE) were selected as packaging material as these are flexible, comparatively cheap, easy to handle and are less permeable to exchange of gases (Kumkum *et al.*, 2010). With increase in storage period enhancement of moisture was observed (Table 29). Nevertheless, this increase in both packaging material was not significant and was within permissible limit of BIS. The increase was higher in HDPE than ALPE which can be reasoned to water vapour transmission property of polyethylene bags (Dabhade and Khedkar, 1980) and to the diffusion of gases and vapour through microscopic pores or by activated diffusion through polyethylene pouch (Palling, 1980). The increase in moisture content of different mixes was also observed by various researchers in malted and roasted supplementary mix

(Banakar, 2005), cereal based weaning mix (Kumkum *et al.,* 2010), little millet and multigrain based composite mix (Kurahatti, 2010) and multigrain based halwa mix (Itagi *et al.,* 2013). The package used was reported to support exchange of gases resulting in leaching of atmospheric humidity into the products (Banakar, 2005). The DPPH radical scavenging activity and total antioxidant activity decreased significantly. However, packaging material did not influence antioxidant capacity only days of storage affected. This probably be due reduction in antioxidant components on storage.

Storage for a long period of six months is expected to produce changes in physical and chemical characteristics of the product. This in-turn might influence sensory quality. Nevertheless, in the present study the packaging material rather than days of storage affected appearance, colour and texture but not taste, flavor and overall acceptability (Fig 15). Aluminum foil coated pouches exhibited better scores of 'liked moderately' to 'liked very much'.

5.9 ANTIDIABETIC PROPERTY OF COMPOSITE MIX

Diabetes mellitus is increasing day by day in India due to changes in life style, faulty food habits, stressful life and of course syndrome X. Type 2 diabetes is the most commonly encountered problem which is associated with postprandial hyperglycemia. It is a disorder caused by a combination of insulin resistance and impaired insulin secretion (Chandalia *et al.,* 2000). The incidence of disease is escalating so as to call India diabetic capital of the world. Though pharmaceutical treatment is inevitable, initial stage of diagnosis calls for dietary means of prescription, besides the medicines involved in treatment of hyperglycemic symptions are expensive and are not devoid of side effects. In the therapeutic management of diabetes, foods having low glycemic index are employed in diet planning. By definition glycemic index is a measure of capacity of food to raise the blood glucose level after consumption (Wolever 1992, Adreson, *et al.,* 2002, Bronus, *et al.,* 2005, and venne, *et al.,* 2007). Lower the glycemic index of a food, slower will be the increase in blood glucose level. It is represented by the increment in the area under the curve of test meal in comparison to standard meal. Ayurvedic system of medicine lists numerous herbal preparations for the management of diabetes mellitus. Many such foods are used ethnopharmacologically to treat symptoms of diabetes and have been studied extensively (Banakar, 2005, Eshwaran *et al.,* 1991, Eshwarani *et al,* 1992 and Subbulakshmi and Naik, 2001).

Fruits and vegetables not only possess a plethora of nutrients but also are a good source of health promoting nutraceuticals like polyphenols, dietary fiber, flavonoids, tannins and others. Hence, it is associated with reduced incidence of cardiovascular diseases, cancer, diabetes mellitus, Alzheimer's disease, cataract and age related diseases.

Prakash *et al.,* (2009) reported the medicinal properties of jackfruit due to the presence of phenolic compounds which when isolated exhibit anti-inflammatory effect. Jackfruit contains prenylflavones which has strong antioxidant property and protects from lipid peroxidation of biological membranes. Ayurvedic treatment of hyperglycemia and diabetes employs extract of mature leaves of jackfruit. Yosuf *et al.,* (2005) while studying glucose response following fruit ingestion reported lower glycemic index of jackfruit. In the present study an attempt was made to develop antidiabetic composite mix based on mature jackfruit flour as mature jackfruit flour contained higher phenols, dietary fiber (Table 28 or Fig 13) and was possessing similar characters like wheat flour (Table 21).

The antidiabetic property of developed composite mix was assessed by testing the inhibitory effect of specific enzymes involved in carbohydrate metabolism. The inhibition of alpha-glucosidase and alpha-amylase, enzymes involved in the digestion of carbohydrates, can significantly reduce the post-prandial increase of blood glucose and therefore can be an important strategy in the management of blood glucose level in type 2 diabetic and borderline patients. Reduction in postprandial hyperglycemia can be achieved by inhibiting the enzymes of intestine involved in glucose metabolism (Aloulou *et al.,* 2012). In the current work, the alpha amylase inhibition of the composite mix was 57 per cent while that of mature jackfruit flour was around 77 per cent. The reduction can be reasoned to the presence of wheat flour in the composite mix along with other spices. However, there was no significant difference in the per cent inhibition of alpha glucosidase by mature jackfruit flour and composite mix. Kifle *et al.,* (2020) reported strongest inhibitory activity by ethyl acetate fraction compared to standard acrobose. Number of studies indicating enzyme inhibition were conducted on extracts (Nair., 2013, Elya, 2015 Ajiboye, *et al.,* 2016 and Hossain, *et al.,* 2018) as against whole meal in the present study. In vitro glycemic index was estimated using the starch digestibility. It was predicted in the present study that the glycemic index of composite mix was 48.47 while that of mature jackfruit flour was 54.75. This can be reasoned to the alpha amylase and alpha glucosidase inhibition. Further, the composite mix contained higher amounts of slow digestible starch and lower amounts of rapid digestible starch (Table 27)

In vivo glycemic index was estimated using non diabetic healthy volunteers of 31-39 years old. It was observed that composite mix had lower glucose response compared to standard (Fig 19). This has resulted in low glycemic index of 40.82 compared to 100 in standard. Jenkins and coworkers (1987) stated that the dietary fibers have role to enfold the food. The dietary fibers hinder the action of hydrolytic enzymes in the gut, increase the viscosity of intestinal contents and thereby reduce the digestion and absorption of carbohydrates, *in vivo*.

5.10 ACCEPTABILITY OF ANTIDIABETIC COMPOSITE MIX BY DIABETIC POPULATION

The ultimatum of any product development is acceptability. Even if a product is highly nutritious and health promoting, unless it is acceptable especially by the target population, the developed product will not serve the purpose. Because food needs to be consumed in higher amounts to offer the requisite benefits, unlike the pharmaceutical preparations, the acceptability of the product by target group becomes essential.

Though the composite mix developed in the present study was accepted by the scientific panel in the laboratory, (table 22). It was felt essential to test the acceptability and receive feedback from the prospective consumers of the developed mix. In the present study one chapathi was offered to diabetic subjects and were instructed to give feedback. Around 81 per cent of the subjects liked it (table 40), nearly 36 percent of the diabetic subjects were ready to eat the mix in the form of chapathi or *thalipattu* now and then. Very less percent of them did not like it. The diabetic subjects had included millets, vegetables, multigrain *atta* and such high fiber food in daily diet with exclusion of simple sugars, sweets and high fat foods (table 39). Further the subjects were of the opinion that it can be consumed in the form of chapathi, dosa, *thalipattu, poori*, and snacks like *sankarpole*, ribbons etc. as an alternate to get the variations in daily diet. On consumption of composite mix chapathi, the subjects expressed feeling of satiety for longer duration and the time of next meal prolonged without cravings for between meal consumptions. Also the chapathi were reported to be soft and pliable with slight after taste which could be ignored looking to the benefits. Further few respondents also reported reducution of 1-2kg of body weight and were feeling light and energetic. Nearly 63 per cent of the diabetic subjects were ready to purchase the mix if made available commercially as it offers convenience in preparations.

Since majority of the subjects follow dietary recommendations of dietitians and doctors, the product can be promoted through hospitals and health clinics. As the computed cost of the mix without profit accounts to Rs. 270/- per kg, it was expressed to be inexpensive by the subjects compared to other products available in the market. Similar results were reported by (Ugare *et al.* 2011) barnyard millet health mix, (Itagi 2003) on the consumption of little and foxtail millet diabetic mix, when worked on barnyard and little millets.

Hence, it can be concluded that the mature jackfruit flour based antidiabetic composite mix having selflife of six months, can be consumed every day in form of chapathi or *thalipattu*. This helps to maintain blood glucose level among diabetic subjects.

Future line of work

❖ Assessment of antioxidant component and activity in different verities of jackfruit

❖ Long term feeding studies of developed composite mix can be undertaken

❖ Popularization of developed antidiabetic composite mix.

CHAPTER -6

BRIEF AND CONCLUSION

Jackfruit belongs to Mulberry family, which possesses nutritional and therapeutic value, in term of beta carotene, other vitamins and phytochemicals besides major nutrients like starch and sugars. The present investigation entitled " Value addition, and therapeutic significance of Jackfruit (*Artocarpus heterophyllus*)" was undertaken in Department of Food Science and Nutrition, College of Community Science, UAS, Dharwad during the year 2015-2017 with the objectives to estimate the nutrient composition of jackfruit at different stages of maturity; to find out the antioxidant activity of jackfruit at various stages of maturity; to design and develop anti-diabetic food product; to characterize the developed product for Glycemic Index, nutritional, sensory, microbial and storage quality; to test the efficacy of developed product among diabetic population.

The salient findings of the investigations are summarized here under.

- Jackfruit was utilized in many ways, all selected subjects (100%) used for self consumption. Sixty eight per cent of the subjects preserved for future use while, 28 per cent of them were involved in commercialization of fruit and fruit products.

- Jackfruit were used in food preparations at different stages of maturity, *Sambhar* and pickle were prepared with young and mature jackfruit. *Dosa, idli* and *paddu* were prepared with both unripe and ripe jackfruit. Jackfruit *bhath* was prepared with young jackfruit. Papad and chips were prepared in mature stage, while, *laddu/modak* were prepared with ripe fruits.

- General methods practiced for the preservation of jackfruit include, pickling (sweet/salty) for young jackfruit. Fresh bulbs of mature jackfruit were preserved in carboys with salt. Jackfruit was preserved as jam or leather in ripe stage. Raw jackfruit seeds were preserved in sun dried form and also as roasted form in air tight container.

- The average length of immature, mature and ripe jackfruit was 11.7 cm, 47.18 cm and 44.2 cm respectively whereas average breadth for same stages was 13.35 cm, 26.12 cm and 25.51 cm respectively.

- The percentage of inedible and edible portions of mature and ripe jackfruit was 32.76 and 56.96, 59.28 and 28.51 respectively.

- The moisture content of jackfruit in the three stages viz. immature, mature and ripe was 70.61, 68.43 and 76.20 respectively with ripe fruit having significantly higher value (76.20%) and mature having significantly lower (68.43%).

- Protein content was found to be maximum (4.36%) in mature fruit followed by immature fruit (3.42%). Crude fat values (%) for the three stages were 4.16, 2.43 and 1.76 respectively, and was significantly maximum in immature and minimum in ripe fruit.

- The total and available carbohydrates were significantly higher in mature (21.25 & 13.45 respectively) followed by ripe (17.44 & 8.15 respectively) and immature (8.60 & 7.12 respectively) fruits. The energy content (kcal) in the three stages were found to be 86, 124 and 92 respectively, mature having maximum and immature having minimum.

- The calcium content ranged from 36.75 to 55.30 mg/100g; iron ranged from 0.34 to 2.75 mg/100g; zinc from 0.09 to 2.44; copper from 0.20 to 2.00mg/100g. Manganese content of both mature and ripe jackfruit was 0.36mg/100g, whereas immature fruit contained 0.94mg/100g.

- Total, reducing and non-reducing sugars were significantly higher in ripe fruits (13.03, 8.77 & 4.05% respectively) followed by mature (0.40, 0.38 & 1.04% respectively).

- The total starch, amylopectin and resistant starch contents were found to be higher in mature jackfruit (40.50, 32.54 & 16.09% respectively). Resistant starch was significantly lower in immature (8.24%) fruit.

- Total (14.7 %), soluble (9.70 %) and insoluble (5.00 %) dietary fibre was highest in mature jackfruit and digestibility index was significantly higher in ripe jackfruit (49.17 %) followed by immature (28.19 %) and mature fruit (27.84 %).

- Immature jackfruit showed higher amount of total phenols (55.03mgGAE/g) while tannins were observed higher in ripe jackfruit (0.53mgTAE/g).

- The values of DPPH and phosphomolybdenum at immature stage were 98.15 and 70.62 per cent respectively and were significantly higher.

- Lowest glycemic index of 47.66 per cent and glycemic load 3.39 per cent were predicted in immature stage of jackfruit.

- The flour yield, pH and bulk density were 26.84 per cent, 6.20 and 0.65 g/ml respectively and were maximum for mature jackfruit.

- The L, a, b values of mature jackfruit flour (85.86, 2.98 and 13.10 respectively) were nearer to the values of wheat flour (89.87, 1.47 & 10.92 respectively).

- Capacity to absorb water and oil, capacity to swell and solubility were higher in mature jackfruit flour (308.66%, 19.67%, 8.92% and 17.84% respectively).

- Jackfruit flour developed was used to formulate composite mix using other ingredients. Mature jackfruit flour was combined with wheat flour in the ratio of 10:90, 20:80, 30:70, 40:60 and 50:50. Formulation with 50 per cent jack fruit flour with 50 per cent wheat flour was acceptable and good in taste.

- After adding spice mix to the composite mix, chapathi with 30 per cent of composite mix and 70 per cent of wheat flour obtained highest score of 8.09 for appearance, 8.50 for colour, 8.77 for flavour, 7.18 for taste, 7.14 for texture and 8.50 for overall acceptability.

- Flavour of 30:70 chapathi scored significantly higher than control with acceptability index of 89.22 per cent. With increase in the proportion of mature jackfruit flour, sensory scores decreased.

- Composite mix exhibited 'L', 'a', 'b' values of 85.88, 1.97 and 11.92 indicating that composite mix was darker than wheat flour (L-89.87). However, redness and yellowness were lower than mature jackfruit flour ('a'-2.98 and 'b'-13.10).

- Higher proportion (41.88%) of jackfruit based composite mix passed through 85(180μm) mesh BSS standard sieve, followed by 150 (16.76%) and 60 (15.10%).

- Water absorption capacity of composite mix (199.46%) was significantly lower than that of mature jackfruit flour (308.66%) and significantly higher than wheat flour (66.40%).

- On the contrary, oil absorption capacity of composite mix (308.23%) was significantly higher than mature jackfruit flour (19.67%) and was on par with that of wheat flour (310.77%).

- Composite mix had higher swelling capacity of 49.70 per cent while wheat flour had swelling capacity of 3.10 per cent, while, mature jackfruit flour had 8.92 per cent. The solubility of composite mix was 11.93 per cent which was significantly lower than that of wheat flour (9.24%) and significantly higher than mature jackfruit flour (17.83%).

- Protein, crude fiber, total and available carbohydrate (13.68, 18.05, 56.96 and 35.11%) were significantly higher in composite mix compared to mature jackfruit flour (4.36, 3.52, 21.25 and 13.45% respectively). Composite mix contained significantly higher energy of 287 kcal while it was 124 kcal in mature jackfruit flour.

- Starch digestibility of antidiabetic composite mix was observed to be highest at 90 min (11.53%) followed by 120 min (10.98%) and lower at 30 min (6.89%) while the digestibility in mature jackfruit flour was highest (19.35%) at 120 min followed by 90 (12.76%) and 30 min (12.53%).

- Soluble, insoluble and total dietary fibre was recorded to be significantly higher in composite mix (7.16, 14.70 and 21.68% respectively) compared to mature jackfruit flour (5.00, 9.70 and 14.70% respectively).

- Composite flour exhibited higher amounts of polyphenols 90.16 mg GAE/g and tannins (89.40 mgTAE/g) compared to mature jackfruit flour (53.10 mg GAE/g and 0.41 mgTAE/g).

- The DPPH and phosphomolybdenum inhibition were significantly higher in composite mix (96.00% &79.00 % respectively) compared to mature jackfruit flour (67.41% & 61.43% respectively).

- Antidiabetic composite mix was packed in polyethylene and aluminium foil coated pouches and stored at ambient temperature for a period of six months. The moisture content of freshly prepared product was 8.24 per cent which increased to 11.23 per cent in high density polyethylene and to 10.72 per cent in aluminium foil coated pouches, at the end of storage (180 day) period.

- DPPH (2,2-diphenyl-1-picryl-hydrazyl-hydrate) inhibition was 96 per cent at the beginning of storage period which reduced to 85.76 and 86.45 per cent after 180th day of storage in aluminium foil and high density polyethylene packages respectively.

- Mean of two per cent reduction in DPPH inhibition was recorded in case of both the packaging and near 2.6 per cent reduction was observed in total antioxidant capacity in both the packaging during the storage period.

- When freshly prepared only one colony of bacteria was detected in the mix and it increased to 27.20 and 26.76 CFU/g in aluminium foil and high density polyethylene packages respectively after 180 days of storage. The increase was higher in aluminium foil package compared to HDPE.

- The fungal count were not detected when freshly prepared but increased to 8.25 and 8.45 CFU/g at the end of storage period of 180 days. It was noticeable that E. coli were not detected even after 180 days of storage in both packaging materials tested and Actinomycetes was also not present.

- Antidiabetic property in terms of inhibition of alpha amylase was significantly lower in composite mix (57.00) than in mature jackfruit flour (77.44). However, alpha glucosidase inhibition was similar in both composite mix and mature jackfruit flour (64.00 and 64.72% respectively).

- The glycemic index was predicted to be 48.47 in composite mix and 54.75 in mature jackfruit flour.

- Mean fasting blood glucose was 91.62 mg/dl for glucose tolerance test, which increased to 148.87mg/dl after 30 min and to 161.62 mg/dl after 60 min of feeding. Further, a decline was observed till 120 min to nearly basal level (96.75mg/dl).

- On the test meal fasting blood glucose was 95.25mg/dl which increased to 117.87mg/dl after 30 min of feeding and to 122.50 mg/dl after 60 min. Later a decrease was observed to 93.63mg/dl after 120min.

- Glycemic index of developed antidiabetic composite mix was 48.47 which falls in low GI category and glycemic load was 14.33, which lie under medium glycemic load category.

- To know the acceptability of developed product among target groups, 31 subjects were selected, where 62 per cent were males and 38 per cent were females. Mean age of male subjects was 54±6.49 years ranging between 46 to 65 years while that of females was 53±3.95 years ranging between 48 to 63 years.

- The food habits and consumption pattern of diabetic subjects depicted that, majority (67.75%) of the subjects modified their normal diet. Around 48 per cent of the subjects were following diet recommended by dietician whereas, 28.57 and 23.80 per cent of them were practicing recommendations of doctor and self-modification respectively.

- Foods included, restricted and avoided by the diabetic subjects selected for acceptability of composite mix are stevia powder, aloe vera juice, *noni* juice, amla, menthe seeds and papaya leaf juice whereas less number of subjects were including multigrain seeds followed by nigella seeds and least number of subjects had included wheat grass juice, *jamun* seed juice, bitter gourd, *sadabahar* leaves juice, banana flower respectively. Foods avoided are rice, wheat, *chapathi, payasa,* jaggery, potatoes, white sugar, sweets and fried foods.

- All the subjects excluded potato, white sugar, sweets and fried foods. Around 90.00 and 84.00 per cent of the respondents avoided payasa and rice respectively. More than 25.00 per cent of the respondents included stevia powder and Aloevera juice. Around 19.00 per cent of the respondents included noni and amla juice.

- The biochemical parameters like haemoglobin ranged from 10.00 to 14.50 g/dl with mean value of 12.00±1.15 g/dl.

- The range of fasting and post prandial blood glucose was 110 mg/dl to 307 mg/dl and 154 to 275 mg/dl respectively with mean value of 129.00 mg/dl and 186.00 mg/dl. HBA1C ranged from 6.1 to 10.2 per cent. Systolic blood pressure ranged from 180 to 110 mmHg mean value of systolic was 131.00 mmHg and diastolic ranged from and 70 to 110 mmHg with mean value of 83.71 mmHg.

- Knowledge of selected subjects regarding diabetes portrayed that, 67.74 per cent of the subjects had knowledge about diabetes while, 32.25 per cent of them did not have any knowledge about the disease.

- The maximum number (35.48%) of the respondents said that they like the jackfruit based composite mix and would eat it often.

- Estimated cost per kg of jackfruit flour was 270.00 and 185.00 when 5 kg or 50 kg was prepared and per kg of mature jackfruit based antidiabetic composite mix was 272.00 and 185.00 when 5 kg or 50 kg was prepared.

Hence, it can be concluded that jackfruit at three different stages of maturity contain significantly different amount of nutrients and antioxidants. Immature and mature jackfruit falls under low glycemic index whereas ripe jackfruit lies under medium glycemic index. Mature jackfruit can be successfully processed and converted in to flour. Up to 50 per cent of mature jackfruit flour can be incorporated in wheat flour along with spices. Glycemic index of designed antidiabetic composite mix was lower than mature jackfruit flour. *In-vivo* and *in-vitro* estimation of glycemic index of composite mix was similar to each other. Proximate princilpes, antioxidants, antidiabetic activity of developed composite mix was higher when compared with mature jackfruit flour. Developed product can be stored up to 180 days at ambient temperature in aluminium coated pouches or in high density polyethylene pouches, without much change in chemical and sensory parameter. Anti-diabetic, mature jackfruit based composite mix was highly accepted among diabetic population who were 2 to 7 years of diabetic. Price the cost of mature jackfruit flour and developed composite mix are not very high which is around Rs 270/- kg.